Land Your Dream Job in Portland

(and Beyond)

The Complete Mac's List Guide

Land Your Dream Job in Portland

(and Beyond)

The Complete Mac's List Guide

First Edition

Mac's List • 620 SW Fifth Avenue, Suite 702 • Portland, OR 97204

Land Your Dream Job in Portland (and Beyond)
The Complete Mac's List Guide

Publisher: Mac's List
President: Mac Prichard
Managing Director: Ben Forstag
Editorial and Production Manager: Kris Swanson, Swanson Editorial Services, Inc.
Design and Layout: Hilary Hudgens and Sarah Reed, Hilary Hudgens Design
Illustrations: Andrew Grewell
Photos: Dreamstime; Fotolia; iStock;
Portland-Milwaukie Light Rail Transit Project / TriMet, www.trimet.org;
RF123, ShutterStock
Copyeditor/Proofreader: Tanya Hanson

ISBN: 978-0-9909551-2-2

Mac's List
620 SW Fifth Avenue, Suite 702 • Portland, OR 97204 • USA
Mac's List is Portland's top source for jobs in the city and throughout Oregon.
Its mission is to help people throughout Oregon find rewarding, interesting
jobs that pay decent salaries and to help employers find the best possible
candidates for those jobs.

Table of Contents

Introduction

Looking for work in Oregon?

We've done it ourselves and helped thousands of others. We can help you, too *(but get ready to hustle).*

Whether you are a longtime resident or a recent transplant, Oregon is an exciting place to live and work. Data from United Van Lines shows that the Pacific Northwest and Northern California were its two most popular destinations in 2013, with Portland among the top six cities experiencing the greatest number of new arrivals.

As you probably know, Portland has been undergoing unprecedented growth as it solidifies its reputation as a hub for millenials, young families, empty nesters, retirees, creatives, and all-around aficionados of public transportation, cycling, innovative cuisine, urban living, green spaces, the arts, the great outdoors, dogs, coffee, and craft beers, to name just a few of its many attractions.

Unfortunately, all that wonderfulness is accompanied by a highly competitive job market. As the old state tourism slogan says, "Oregon! Things look different here." That also holds true when it comes to finding employment. While job markets have been slow across the entire United States, the unemployment rate in Oregon has long remained higher than the average. (At the end of 2013, Oregon ranked thirty-second in a listing of unemployment rates in all states, with fiftieth as the highest.)

According to a recent study* by two Portland State University researchers, Jason Jurjevich, PhD, and Greg Schrock, PhD, Portland has attracted and retained young college graduates at some of the highest levels in the country in spite of fewer local job opportunities. In addition, empty nesters and retirees (age forty and up) have been arriving in Portland at higher-than-expected rates. This all adds up to more competition for fewer jobs, especially jobs that require highly educated applicants.

So, keeping all that in mind, looking for work in Oregon requires determination, strategic thinking, and the ability to adapt to local conditions. That's where the expertise of the people at Mac's List comes in.

Mac's List began in 2001, when founder Mac Prichard started sharing local job postings with a few dozen friends and people looking for work. As the years went by, this list grew by word of mouth as he heard from people who wanted to join his list and employers who asked him to post their jobs. By 2008, emailing all the job announcements had become an unpaid part-time job for Mac. The list had reached

850 people, and the number of positions grew to ten or fifteen a week. It had also become an important community service. To reduce the amount of work involved—and to keep connecting job seekers and employers— Mac's colleague, Lori Howell, suggested publishing a list of each week's jobs as a simple curated newsletter every Tuesday at 2:00 p.m.

Mac's List still publishes a newsletter each Tuesday, with (on average) over a hundred new jobs for career-minded professionals. It has also added new services including a website, a career development blog, networking events, and dedicated Twitter, Facebook, LinkedIn, YouTube, Instagram, and Pinterest. The website attracts tens of thousands of visitors every month and has evolved to meet the demands of its readers and the employers who want to connect with them.

One thing that hasn't changed since 2001 is its goal of providing valuable and consistent information about Oregon jobs in management, communications, development, and other sectors and professions. Its central mission has also remained unchanged: to help people throughout Oregon find rewarding, interesting jobs that pay reasonable salaries and to help employers find the best possible candidates for those jobs.

This book combines information from the Mac's List blog with job-hunting tips from local experts, many of whom have been and continue to be valuable contributors to the blog. It provides a chapter-by-chapter guide to finding a job in Oregon, as well as tips for managing your employment goals across your career.

You've made the decision to look for work in Oregon. Now it's time to get inspired and acquire the job-hunting skills and expertise you need. An investment of time and energy now in your career and in yourself will pay big dividends in the not-so-distant future.

You can do it! Ready ... set ... and ... GO!

Mac Prichard: How I Found a Job in Oregon

Mac's List founder and president of Prichard Communications

In 1991, my wife Kris and I were living in Boston, where I was finishing up a master's degree in public administration. After almost a decade in New England, we wanted to try a new location and we were attracted by Oregon's quality of life.

By July of that year, I'd accepted a position as city hall communications director for Earl Blumenauer, now a member of Congress, but then a Portland city commissioner about to run for mayor of Portland in 1992.

How did I find a job in Portland while living in Boston—2,536 miles away? Here's what worked for me.

Know your goals. I had a specific job objective: I wanted a senior communications or policy staff position with an Oregon elected official, a political campaign, or a university. Having a well-defined goal helped me determine whom to call for informational interviews and made it easier for people to share contacts and leads.

Use your networks. I tapped into every network I could—family, friends, classmates, alumni, and colleagues. It was surprising how many of my best contacts in Oregon came to me from people I knew in Boston or in the Midwest where I grew up.

Informational interviews work. If I relied on publicly advertised job postings alone back in '91, I would still be in Boston. The best opportunities I discovered, including the one I accepted at city hall, were never advertised. Doing informational interviews allowed me to introduce myself to employers and learn about upcoming positions.

People will help you. During my six-month job search I reached out to more than 100 people. Many were busy and prominent: the speaker of the Oregon House of Representatives, the governor's chief of staff, and state and local elected officials. In spite of packed calendars, almost all made time to see and help me. I can count on one hand the number who said no.

Homework pays off. Even in the pre-Internet days of 1991, there were many books, people, and even rudimentary online resources available to me in Boston that I used to research possible Portland employers and people I might contact for informational interviews. Doing that kind of research made my search more efficient and gave me an edge in job interviews.

You'll make many friends along the way. It's a cliché, but it's true: every city is a small town. Since moving to Oregon twenty-four years ago, I've had a rewarding communications career working with nonprofits, government agencies, and elected officials. Many of the people I met here during my first job search in 1991 became coworkers, colleagues, and good friends.

Acknowledgments

We would like to extend a hearty "Thank you!" to all the people who have contributed to the Mac's List blog and to the content of this guide in particular. We get so many great ideas and suggestions from the Mac's List community, and your comments and feedback constantly shape the topics we write about. You are an important part of what we do!

Extra special thanks go to the local experts who contributed content to this guide: Brittany Bennett, Satya Byock, Jennie Day-Burget, Aubrie De Clerck, Linda Favero, Jenny Foss, Vicki Lind, Gabrielle Nygaard, Dawn Rasmussen, Mike Russell, Laura Schlafly, Jen Violi, Joshua Waldman, Marsha Warner, and Mara Woloshin. You rock!

We are also grateful to the other experts whose suggestions and advice we have referenced or quoted in these pages. Be sure to check them out and learn more about them in the resource links that appear at the end of each chapter!

Many thanks as well to the former Prichard Communications and Mac's List staff and interns whose blog posts and editorial expertise have helped shape the content of this guide. We are grateful for your contributions!

We are especially appreciative of the excellent work done by our editorial and design team. A big thank you goes out to writer and editor Kris Swanson of Swanson Editorial Services, who kept us in line and was occasionally nice about it; designers Hilary Hudgens and Sarah Reed of Hilary Hudgens Design, of which only one is a woman; illustrator Andrew Grewell, who knows more about goats than you do; and copyeditor and proofreader Tanya Hanson, who loves a well-placed semicolon.

And finally, another round of thanks to you, our readers. Keep those comments and suggestions coming! We want to know what you think. Please contact us at: info@macslist.org and let us know what's on your mind.

The Mac's List Team: Mac Prichard and Ben Forstag

1 Assessing Your Interests and Skills

Don't be afraid to get naked!

The World Naked Bike Ride is an annual ride organized around the world to "draw attention to oil dependency and the negative social and environmental impacts of a car-dominated culture." In Portland the ride is celebrated with great enthusiasm, while police urge the thousands of riders to at least wear shoes and helmets for safety's sake. In a town that celebrates nudity (who can forget former mayor Bud Clark's famous "Expose Yourself to Art" poster, which depicts him flashing a downtown statue), the ride is the ultimate example of letting it all hang out—the "good," the "bad," and the "hasn't-seen-the-sun-in-almost-a-year ugly."

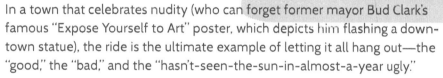

Before you can find the perfect job, you need to take a good, hard look at yourself, your loves and hates, and your strengths and weaknesses. Begin by taking it all off. Strip away any preconceived ideas you might have about what you should do (or what others think you should do) and invest the time in exploring your passions and how you can apply them to your job search.

Do the analytical work.

There's no way around it. You've got to do the work if you want to do an honest self-assessment. Whether you are looking for your first job, searching for a new job, or changing careers, you need to commit to this step and remember that time and effort now will save time and effort down the line.

For most people, the key to happiness in any career is to find a workplace that shares their values and a job that allows them to use their strengths. So the question is, where to begin?

Take advantage of existing resources. Luckily there are many tools and informational materials designed to help you answer these questions. These three are favorites here at Mac's List:

- *Strengths Finder 2.0* by Tom Rath: Do you ever wonder why you sometimes finish a task feeling exhausted and depleted, yet other days you walk away with a strong sense of self-worth and satisfaction of a job well done? Chances are that on the exhausted days, you didn't get to use your strengths. On the days when you're in the flow, you were able to use your talents toward a job well done. (Bonus: If you buy the book, you get an access code to take an online assessment, which takes about thirty minutes.)

- *What Color Is Your Parachute? A Practical Manual for Job Hunters and Career Changers* by Richard Bolles: Yes, it was first published in 1970 and has had over forty editions since then, but it still remains an invaluable tool for professional self-discovery. Doing the exercises helps to uncover new ideas and to reveal potential areas for informational interviews, exploration, and research. It's a great career guide and self-discovery tool all in one.

- *The Career Guide for Creative and Unconventional People by Carol Eikleberry:* Exploring your strengths can lead you down several different career paths, so you may need to get creative in your search for happiness at work. This book can help you identify opportunities that you may never have thought of.

Ask yourself the hard questions. Is quality of life more important to you than a large paycheck? Do you hate teamwork? Do you love networking or dislike sitting in an office? Do you want to do different things every day? What are your passions? What are your values? Where do you see yourself in five years? In ten years? An honest self-assessment gives you the opportunity to reflect on your answers to these and similar questions.

It's All About You!

by **Linda Favero** Organization + Individual Development

Knowing yourself is the first step in the job search process. Answer the following questions to begin your own self-assessment process.

What do you do best?

- Your skills, knowledge, and competencies are acquired through education and experience of all kinds (employment, volunteer work, life experience, and so on). They represent your principal assets in the job market, so an important part of communicating your value is correctly identifying and labeling these skills.

- Your personal characteristics or adaptive skills are inborn or developed early in life. They can include abilities, talents, or a predisposition to certain career directions.

- Your accomplishments are the things you've done that you are most proud of.

What do you like to do?

- Your interests should help shape your professional objective, which should be something you are interested in as well as something you are good at.

- Your values are your core beliefs about what is most important in life. They usually evolve slowly and may change across your life.

What are your priorities in life?

- Your personal preferences are things such as location, schedules, and income. Your professional objective should be consistent with your career vision and lifestyle needs.

- Your motivation consists of the drivers or needs that propel you along in your chosen career direction, such as a sense of accomplishment, the satisfaction of being part of a team, or the desire to travel.

Where do you fit? Although you may appreciate a good wage, you should also consider many other factors, especially when working in Portland.

- **Culture:** Do you want a clear line of command or something less hierarchical?
- **Wellness:** Does the company offer yoga? Encourage noontime runs? Discount gym memberships?
- **Global opportunities:** Do you like to travel to the far reaches of the planet or hang close to home?
- **Workspace:** Have you dreamed of the corner office or do you prefer an open environment with bean bag chairs?
- **Flexibility:** Do you need an office to stay focused or do you enjoy the opportunity to work from home?
- **Professional development:** Do you want an MBA or the chance to travel to conferences in sunny spots? (It does get awfully gray here!)

Explore your strengths and weaknesses in other ways. Sometimes a more tangential approach can yield productive insights and results. (See end-of-chapter resource list.)

- **Breitenbush Hot Springs Retreat and Conference Center** is a yoga, meditation, and higher-learning center in Detroit, Oregon, about two hours outside of Portland. It's a great place for a weekend workshop, a relaxing day of reflection soaking in the pools, or a cabin getaway.
- **Writing workshops** can help unleash your creativity and foster self-reflection. The Attic Institute on SE Hawthorne Boulevard offers a variety of options.
- **Volunteer service programs** are available through many organizations that offer volunteer opportunities in exchange for room and board.
- **Travel with a purpose** can help build self-knowledge, especially when you connect with organizations that combine travel and volunteer opportunities.
- **Community classes** can broaden your horizons and help you explore new realms. For example, Portland Community College offers great opportunities for creative learning as well as career assessment and development.

Wander with intention. "Not all who wander are lost," and, as noted above, sometimes the journey off the beaten path may turn out to be more rewarding than one that follows a straight line. So don't get too hung up on having to move directly from point A to point B. The main thing is to continue the journey and be mindful about your experiences. If you follow your inclinations with deliberate thought and analysis, you will learn a lot about yourself along the way.

Pay attention to your emotions.

While your head is engaged in thought, reflection, and analysis, you also need to listen to what your heart is telling you. Don't tune out your emotions—both positive and negative—and try to see what you can learn from both your passions and your fears.

Identify your passions and be realistic about them. Do you say you are passionate about running but never go for a run? Do you claim to be passionate about cooking but never cook? Stop fooling yourself. Whatever you spend most of your time doing—that's your passion.

Show passion in your job search. Volunteer for your passion, network where your passion is, do informational interviews in the fields where you are passionate, or take classes related to your passion. Do you really care about the environment? Let it shine in your interview—it shows personality, enthusiasm, and commitment to a cause—all valuable traits in any employee.

Combine your passions with your strengths. Are you great with numbers but passionate about saving animals? If you get a job as an accountant at an animal welfare nonprofit, will working for your cause and being surrounded by like-minded people be enough? Maybe yes, maybe no. You need to think it through in greater detail. Maybe you want to transition into a new skill altogether to pursue your passions?

Manage your fears and negative emotions. If you are doing an open and honest self-assessment, you are also opening a Pandora's Box. Some of the emotions that fly out will be negative ones. Acknowledge them and deal with them openly and directly by doing the following.

- **Be kind to yourself.** According to the Dalai Lama, "If you want others to be happy, practice compassion. If you want to be happy, practice compassion." Kindness and self-acceptance are both the means and the end. Sometimes life just doesn't work out like we hoped it would. You graduate from college and it takes six months to find a paid gig. You divorce at age twenty-nine. You second-guess getting your MBA instead of traveling. We all have decisions we regret and mistakes we've made. Stop beating yourself up; it's unproductive and self-defeating. Accept where you are right now in the present moment.

- **Be mindful and accept uncertainty.** Suffering stems from the stories we tell ourselves, our attachments and aversions, and our inability to accept uncertainty. We cling to the past because it's a known entity, and we try to predict and plan for the future so as to alleviate uncertainty. Accept the uncertainty that is the job search by bringing your attention to the present moment. Drop your awareness into the here and now. Be in the moment. Pet your dog. Meditate. Run. Hike. Surf. Whatever you do, do it with your whole heart and your whole attention. This will allow for the anxiety to soften and the bigger picture to unfold.

- **Be your own friend.** This means treating yourself as you would a best friend. Notice how you talk to yourself. Would you speak that way to a loved one? Not very likely, is it? Give yourself support, the same way you would a close friend. In the end, wherever you go, there you are, so learn to be kind to yourself because you are your own best ally. If you made a mistake, take mental note of what you'll do differently next time and forgive yourself for that mistake.

- **Be active.** Whatever form of exercise you enjoy, make room for it in your schedule. Regular exercise clears your head and elevates your mood.

- **Be generous with your time.** Put your skills to good use and show others what you can do by volunteering. You will come away with new energy as well as terrific contacts, excellent references, and great work samples. And thinking about others will take you outside yourself while giving you a different perspective on your world (and theirs).

Build a community based on your interests.

It's fun and motivational to share your passions and interests with others, and by doing that you are also creating a community of like-minded people who can inform and support your job search along the way.

Seek out others who share your interests. Volunteer or join a Meetup group. Go to a networking event. If you like Frisbee, join an Ultimate team. In need of relaxation and contemplation? Find a yoga studio that feels like home. Whatever it is, make sure it is something you are passionate about or are interested in exploring.

Support those connections. Connect with others, connect your new friends with old friends, and connect their friends with your friends. Support your community and it will support you. Portland fosters this kind of interaction with its creative thinkers and pioneer spirit. Many people here believe that when you give to others, it will surely come back to you. That's the lesson here. Follow this motto for your Portland job search and we'll all be better off for it.

Start something. Don't wait for others to act or to be chosen. Portland has a strong DIY culture and welcomes people who launch their own projects and invite others to join them. Post an announcement on Meetup, ask to make an announcement at the monthly meeting of a professional group, or publish a manifesto on your blog. You may be amazed by who responds.

Advice From an In The Know Portland Expert

Three Tips to Thrive in the Transition from College to Career

by **Satya Byock**, MA, LPC Portland Psychotherapist,
Owner of Quarter-Life Counseling

Congratulations, college graduate! You've worked hard and can now look back on years of schooling and say, "Phew! I made it! But ... now what?"

This next phase of life can be difficult, and the transition into the working world doesn't come with a lot of guidance. Unfortunately, you may have to figure it out largely on your own.

Here are three tips to help you transition smoothly into this next phase of life.

1. **Acknowledge that you're in a transition.** If you're lost at sea and someone asks where you're going, it's only foolishness that wouldn't announce: "I don't quite know!"

   If you don't know where you're headed at the moment, go ahead and admit it. Being honest will take a load off your shoulders, and it will tip off helpful people in your network to your need for support.

   Find a way to speak about your transition with confidence.

   Mom's friend: So what are you up to now that college is over?
   You: Well, I'm taking a breather from the stress of school, and I'm sorting through what's next ...

   Then share about what you are doing: your creative and social life, the job you may have (even if you don't love it). People are going to be asking you all the time what you're up to. Don't let these questions get you down.

2. **Create an accountability group.** If you have ideas of what's next but could use some help getting there, your friends are likely in the same boat. Get together!

   With good food and levity, convene with others to share your goals. Encourage discussion and supportive ideas. Have someone take notes. In two weeks, meet again. Check in on the progress you've made and set new goals. This creates accountability for all of you, and it will help move you closer to the life you're seeking.

   Share your big ambitions, but try to focus on the small goals to get you there: "I want to meet with three people in the design industry," or "I want to write two entries on my cooking blog." Great!

   Remember, a journey of a thousand miles begins with a single step. Supporting these small steps with friends provides incentive to stay on course and keeps unhelpful isolation from taking hold.

3. **Journal.** Your deep self is your own greatest guide. Find some time to write your thoughts and dreams during the week. With each entry, listen to what you're wishing for and striving after. Look for themes.

   You're a unique person with unique interests. As you continue to get to know yourself, the patterns that emerge will begin to shed light on your path ahead.

Address your weaknesses by polishing your skills.

Once you've finished your self-assessment and have a better understanding of your passions, your dislikes, your strengths, and your weaknesses, it's time to see how they match up to the needs of the marketplace. What does today's job market demand of qualified applicants? How many of those skills do you already have? What others do you need to acquire?

Many recruiters and hiring professionals tend to divide skills loosely into hard skills (tangible skills that can be easily learned) and soft skills (more intangible skills that relate to how people interact in the workplace).

Master these hard skills. Kimberlee Stiens, the *Business for Good, Not Evil* blogger, recommends the following skills because they apply to many kinds of jobs in many different areas. Do you have them? Do you need them? (If you need to brush up, check the resource links at the end of this chapter.)

- **Coding:** The marketplace rewards those who understand and can perform basic HTML and CSS coding. With beginner's knowledge you can tweak a website, customize a blog, or make adjustments to online images.

- **Graphic design:** In many offices, some employees double as graphic designers who can work in programs such as InDesign and Photoshop. If you can modify a photo, create a rate card, build a professional binder, and so on, you can do simple design projects on your own.

- **Public speaking:** Scared of speaking in front of others? Join a group like Toastmasters that allows you to practice in front of a supportive group and build your confidence.

- **Writing:** Good writers are keepers in the workforce. Learn to write for the web and social media so that you are concise and practiced in the art of engaging others and you'll be a success at your new job.

- **Advanced Excel:** Many of us play "phone a friend" when it comes to Excel. How about you? How many times have you looked at Excel and thought, "If only I knew how to merge and sort these files?" Get rid of Excel anxiety and take a class. Your new employer will be impressed and your friends will thank you.

Work toward acquiring soft skills. These skills are harder to pinpoint, but it is their very subtlety that makes them so valuable in the workplace. Potential employers pick up on soft skills through nonverbal cues, previous accomplishments, and references from people they know. In fact, many Oregon readers tell us that they found work from relationships that they cultivated and from people in their network. How many of the following soft skills do you have? How many do you need to acquire?

- **Maintaining relationships:** People hire people they know or who are recommended to them by people they trust. Word of mouth is key in many businesses. To get it, a company or organization must have good and trusted relationships with colleagues and customers. Their future success depends on finding employees who know how to do this, too.

- **Working in teams:** Today's workplace demands collaboration. Businesses highly value staff members who work well with others, especially across different organizations, and so do their clients.

- **Staying flexible:** For many American workers, the era of big, bureaucratic organizations is over. Even at large employers, priorities can change quickly. Today's customers expect organizations to be nimble and able to turn on a dime.

- **Learning:** These days everyone has to be a lifelong learner. Job candidates who join professional groups, attend webinars and workshops, and monitor the latest newsletters and blogs stand out and impress potential hirers.

- **Listening:** Sometimes people—colleagues or customers—don't know what they want or have trouble explaining a need or idea. One of the most valuable assets any company can have is staff who know how to listen to others, draw people out, and help everybody understand each other. Divas and monologists? Not so useful.

Stay current. Every year, major trend forecasters predict what will be the most critical skill sets for the coming year. Stay up to date with these lists and keep your job-hunting skills fresh. For example, Meghan Casserly at *Forbes* magazine recently wrote about ten skills the CareerBuilder website identified as key. Note that they are a mix of both hard and soft skills: critical thinking, complex problem solving, judgment and decision making, active listening, computers and electronics, mathematics, operations and systems analysis, monitoring, programming, and sales and marketing.

Dig deeper!

For links to some of the topics covered in this chapter (including mindfulness, essential workplace skills, self kindess and success, courses in coding and graphic design, career transitions, and the Annual Naked Bike Ride, among many others), go to www.macslist.org/references.

Presenting Yourself Online

*Practice shameless
self-promotion!*

Portland's patented weirdness
is well known, but what's hot
today can be history the next.
Take a cue in self-promotion
from Portland's own Belmont Goats. Hired to mow a field on an empty lot
at SE Belmont and 10th Avenue, they became hugely popular as Portland's
original urban goat herd and drew visitors from all over the area. When the
lot was scheduled for redevelopment, herd members Carl, Phil, Chester,
Lefty, Bailey, Dusty, Duchess, Hickory, Bambi, Cooper, Clover, Precious, Atho,
and Winter had to find a new publicly accessible home—and are now keeping
their fans informed about their new location in the Lents neighborhood via
their own website and Facebook page.

*Before you begin contacting and networking with people as part of your job
search, make sure your online house is in order. You need to be virtually visible—
but only in the best way possible. Do an audit of your online presence and work to
eliminate the negative while accentuating the positive. Along the way you'll acquire
new skills, such as using social media, joining professional networking websites,
and practicing etiquette online.*

Clean up your act.

Looking for a job? "You should take care that your social media personality won't
kill your job prospects," says career coach Melissa Anzman, of the *Launch Yourself*
blog. Employers have admitted long ago that they check out job applicants online
as part of the hiring process.

In spite of this common hiring practice, many people say and do things on the Internet that could hurt their next job search. Consider your Twitter feed, Instagram profile, Pinterest page, and Vine account as places where people can get a sense of your personality, all without ever having met you or spoken to you in person. Here's how to make sure that they get a good first impression, not a bad one.

Think like an employer. Do what every human resource manager does: search your name and see what turns up. Then drill down. Although most people don't go beyond the first page of organic search results, you can't always count on this. Don't just search your name; search any previous names, nicknames, or other handles that could be traced back to you. You might be surprised by what pops up.

Don't limit yourself to Google. Use Bing, too, and visit the social networking sites where you have accounts as well as the websites and blogs where you've written under your own name. Clear your browser's data or open a private or "incognito" window to see what a stranger would see when viewing your online identity. Does the material reflect what you want an employer to think about you? Look at your digital footprint from the perspective of a potential employer.

Clean up your online profile. Take action when you find unflattering material. Remove tags from Facebook photos and posts that you don't want shared. Do the same with other social media sites and online platforms. If you can't delete the content yourself, write to the owner of the account, blog, or website, and ask him or her to do it for you. Do your utmost to have it made private or deleted, but be polite about it—shooting off an irritated email could backfire.

Strengthen your privacy settings. Privacy settings for social media accounts can be complicated. Take the time to master them. Privacy options seem not only to change every two weeks but to get more complex. Check your visibility settings often and then check them twice to ensure your online accounts present a positive public image.

Think ahead. Next time, resist the urge to post that rant or send that dicey Snapchat. Consider adding a respected mentor (a judgmental relative will work in a pinch) to your social networks to keep your future posts in line. "When in doubt, leave it out" is the golden rule for maintaining a squeaky-clean online presence.

Polish your online presence.

Once you get rid of as much of the bad as you can, it's time to improve your online persona.

Use SEO tactics to push down the bad news and raise the good. Sometimes you can't make embarrassing content go away, but you can make it harder to find with simple search engine optimization (SEO) techniques. Try to solve the problem yourself before you turn to the booming online reputation management industry. Easy tactics include blogging on professional topics and completing personal profiles for different social media services. As Mac Prichard, Mac's List founder and president of Prichard Communications, says, "Take it from someone who's never had the luxury of hiding behind a common name: there's only so much you can do to wipe yourself off the face of the Web. At that point, go on the offensive. Create a professional website, blog, or Twitter account, and start putting out material you'd *want* employers to see."

Make sure you have a robust online presence. In today's workplace, you must be found digitally in multiple places in order to maintain a level of professional credibility. If you can't be found online, employers will assume you haven't kept up with the times. Be involved with blogs in your field, whether as a writer or a named commenter. Starting your own blog, Facebook group, or website will help boost your online presence in a positive way.

Create an attractive online personality. According to a CareerBuilder survey, more than one-third of employers (thirty-seven percent) now use social networks to screen potential job candidates. Maintaining your online persona is one of the newer skills that job seekers must possess. Use this opportunity to show multiple aspects of your experience and personality, both professional and personal. Your passions make you an attractive employee in the eyes of potential employers—just make sure all the interests and hobbies you mention are neutral and unlikely to offend.

Stay active online. It's not enough to burst online with a flurry of social media pages, blog posts, and online commentary. You have to update regularly and keep yourself current. Remember, in online time, a month of silence is like disappearing forever. Frequent posts and updates keep you visible and alive in people's minds.

Use online resources to promote your professional identity.

Polishing and enhancing your online presence is a great way to market yourself to potential employers. One of the best ways to do it is to make use of the many available online tools and resources that can help you increase that presence while connecting with other people.

Use LinkedIn. This professional networking website is the granddaddy of all online job search resources. One of the most common requests received from Mac's List readers is: "How can I build a LinkedIn profile to catch the attention of a recruiter or an employer?"

It's a question you should ask yourself, even if you're not looking for work and thinking about what an employer will see when your own LinkedIn page pops up on Google. Your LinkedIn account is more than an online resume or a place to check for job postings. Many professionals now use the site to learn about new coworkers, potential vendors, or possible business partners. Others rely on LinkedIn to share news and ideas with colleagues, customers, and employers.

In a recent survey by Jobvite of more than 1,000 human resource and recruiting professionals, ninety-three percent of respondents say they use LinkedIn to find the right candidate.

LinkedIn has more than 200 million members and is growing rapidly, adding new users at the rate of two per second. How can you stand out in such a crowded community and attract the attention of those you want to know about your accomplishments and abilities? Take the following steps.

- **Show yourself.** A profile page without your picture looks forgotten and stagnant. Pick a good photo. This is your first impression, so make it the right one. As Jeff Haden writes in "6 Steps to a More Marketable LinkedIn Profile" in *Inc.* magazine, "The best photo strikes a balance between professionalism and approachability, making you look good but also real." Don't post a vacation photo. Keep it professional. If you can't afford a studio portrait, ask a friend to take a simple headshot with your smartphone.

- **List all key jobs.** Don't add every part-time gig or summer job you've ever had, but do include the most important and relevant jobs in your career. And don't limit yourself to your current position—a common mistake.

- **Showcase your work.** Did you know that LinkedIn will allow you to link to your websites and your Twitter handle as well as stream recent posts from your WordPress blog? Do you have projects you want to showcase? Use the "Projects" feature of LinkedIn. While most of us have posted a career summary on LinkedIn, "Projects" features your special skills. Be sure to use it to highlight your work.

- **Emphasize results, not duties.** The best resumes describe what a person has accomplished, not just his or her responsibilities. The same is true on LinkedIn. In the "Summary" and "Experience" sections of your profile, talk about the benefits you produced for an employer and include keywords that recruiters may use when searching for candidates.

- **Use the "Skills and Endorsements" section strategically.** You can include up to fifty skills and collect endorsements for each of them from your LinkedIn connections. Think strategically about the strengths you want others to know that you have, and add them now yourself. Don't wait for your LinkedIn connections to add them for you.

- **Ask for endorsements (and give them).** A short two- or three-sentence endorsement from a former supervisor or colleague adds invaluable credibility to your profile. Aim to have at least one endorsement for each job. Also offer to give endorsements to others you know well and whose work you can recommend.

- **Build your network every day.** Don't limit your LinkedIn connections to current or recent coworkers. The larger your network, the easier it is for you to connect with employers and leaders in your field. Add colleagues from past jobs, instructors and students from college and high school, and friends, neighbors, and others you know socially. LinkedIn is also a good way to connect with people you meet professionally. Most people are willing to accept invitations from those they haven't met if they share common professional interests.

- **Send a personal note when connecting.** As Portland author Jenny Foss, aka "Job Jenny," writes in "Your LinkedIn Intervention: 5 Changes You Must Make" in *Forbes* magazine, "Avoid the default text like the plague. Make it personal. Make it specific. Make it clear that you're not the laziest person alive." Also, check the end-of-chapter resources for a list of four tips that local expert Joshua Waldman has for connecting with strangers on LinkedIn.

- **Join a group to engage with others and give back.** LinkedIn has become a popular publishing platform to share business ideas. Set aside time to review your news feed and comment on information your connections have posted. Post your own material, including professional milestones, events you plan to attend, or blog posts you've written. Visit and participate in LinkedIn groups such as Portland Oregon Jobs or Networking Portland. Take the time to explore and join some today!

- **Create a custom URL to publicize your LinkedIn profile.** This tip comes courtesy of Mara Woloshin, a frequent *Mac's List* blogger and principal at Woloshin Communications, Inc. As she points out, the use of a consistent name across all of your social networks builds personal brand awareness.

Advice From an In The Know Portland Expert

Let's Have Coffee ... Online.

by **Joshua Waldman** Author of *Job Searching with Social Media for Dummies* and founder of Oregon-based Career Enlightenment, which offers professional LinkedIn writing services for career-serious professionals

In an age of digital tools, digital meetings, and virtual conferences, it should be no surprise that nowadays people long for more human connections. Asking someone for coffee is the universal language of networking, particularly in Portland where the local coffee is absolutely incredible. So why not have your online presence reflect the quality of the coffee you are about to share with a professional contact?

If someone has taken the time to look at your LinkedIn profile, chances are they want to learn more about you and to get a taste for your personality. Offer other websites for them to explore to keep them interested longer. Try setting up a free About.me site where you can upload a high-res image of yourself and link your other social media profiles in one place.

During my own job search in Portland in 2009, I routinely used my online profiles as launching points for initiating a coffee meeting. There is no better way to advance your career and discover new opportunities than leveraging your online platform to build in-person relationships.

Explore other online professional resources. As Joshua mentions, online profiles are a great place to make connections. But that's not all. You can also use online tools to help you create a personal website, maintain and update a professional bio, or a build a portfolio of your work. You can even take advantage of online resume-building services to help you polish your resume within an inch of its life. (See Chapter 5 for more on personal websites, portfolios, and resumes.)

Advice From an In The Know Portland Expert

Power Up Your Resume Online!

by **Mara Woloshin**, MA, APR (Accredited in Public Relations);
Fellow, Public Relations Society of America;
Principal of Woloshin Communications, Inc.

An updated LinkedIn profile is vital when job hunting in Oregon, but to stand out, especially in markets like Portland's creative community, you need to do more. I'm a big fan of two online resume-building tools: Zerply.com and ResumUP.com. Let me tell you why. (And hat tip to Dave Thompson, public affairs manager at Oregon Department of Transportation, for steering me to these sites.)

Zerply is a wonderful starting place for understanding the value and benefits of online resume building. Started in Tallinn, Estonia in 2011, this global online community for creative professionals maintains an "edgy" Old-World flavor while transforming a standard resume into an eye-catching infographic that lets you present your work and your talent. The Zerply community has a uniquely gentle but edgy philosophy that shapes its career guidance and resources as well. The site also includes multiple social elements, including the ability to access a news stream and analyze stats. Building your resume and profile with Zerply's free resources, including international experts in social media, is like eating a chocolate puff pastry off a silver platter with no calories and no cleanup needed.

Much more American flavored is ResumUP. It is one of the initial Facebook-powered resume apps and contains at least a starting place for good career goal setting. I hope you find it easy to use, because personal goal setting really is one of the most important steps in anyone's career development. (However, I just used it to view examples and did my own goal setting the old-fashioned way— with a pen on yellow-lined paper!)

Add social media to your job-hunting skills.

Like it or not, social media is here to stay. What does this mean for you? If you aren't participating in the conversation, you are definitely missing potential opportunities. Employing social media tactics to aid in your job search is an increasingly smart way to spend your time. Today, social media plays an important role in the decision process for hiring managers.

In addition to using social media to create and enhance your online persona, here are ways to make it a part of your job search.

Demonstrate your social media skills. As companies integrate and grow with social media, knowledge of the platforms will become a desired skill set. Social media can be used in a variety of ways and is great for networking in many types of careers.

Use social media to network. Networking isn't new, and it's the best way to find a job. Social networks have taken the barriers out of contacting and connecting with those in hiring positions. Follow the websites, social networking pages, and company blogs of employers you admire so that you know more about them when you connect with them later. Inquiries don't have to be formal and can revolve around common interests.

Learn to love Twitter (even if you don't already). Recently the Paris-based data analysis company Semiocast estimated that more than 500 million people are now using Twitter, with more than 140 million here in the United States alone. Take advantage of its reach and create a Twitter strategy for your Portland job search by following these tips.

- **Use advanced search and know the hashtags for your job search.** Joshua Waldman recommends going to search.twitter.com and performing an advanced search for the word "hiring" within your zip code area. (Waldman says that the number-one hashtag is #hiring, but also look at the end-of-chapter resources for his comprehensive list of fifty hashtags for job searches to cover all your bases.) Mac's List always tags its job openings with #pdxjobs, and so do many local employers. Another good hashtag for learning about job announcements in Oregon is #orjobs.

- **Follow other handles strategically and specifically for job search purposes.** Some universities and university departments, such as The University of Oregon School of Journalism and Communications Career Services Department, are active in the job-search conversation on Twitter. Find tweets about jobs, articles, and events relevant to your local job search in Portland and in Oregon at large.

- **Follow industry leaders.** Stay ahead of the competition. Know the latest trends and issues for your industry by following local leaders in your area of interest.

- **Be strategic in deciding whom to follow online.** Besides finding and interacting with leaders in your professional niche, check out these five local Twitter accounts that the Mac's List team follows to learn about Oregon job openings and career resources:

    @bolywelch tweets daily about Portland networking events and job openings, as well as Oregon economic trends. It is operated by Boly:Welch, a Portland-based employment and executive search agency.

    @larryinpdx provides news about tech jobs in Oregon. Larry Williams isn't a recruiter or a career counselor—he's the director of Web services for the Oregon Entrepreneurs Network—but he frequently tweets about Oregon business and the state's economy and also includes links to job openings in the area.

    @LinfieldCareer was created for Linfield College students and graduates and contains career tips from national bloggers as well as local position listings useful to any professional or job seeker. It is managed by the Linfield Career Hub.

    @PSUCareerCenter publicizes links to national and local blogs, websites, and other job-hunting resources and is offered by Portland State University's Career Center.

    @WorkingChoices tweets local job listings, resources, and links to *The Working Choices Daily*. It's run by the employment program of the Cascade AIDS Project.

Mind your manners online!

It all started with a tweet. A comment on a blog led to an email exchange. You liked my Facebook update, and I thumbs-upped your Instagram photo. Five months later, I've developed an impression of you even though we've never met in person or talked on the phone. Is it a good one?

More and more we create and grow professional and personal relationships in the digital space. This happens every day as email takes the place of a phone call and Google Hangout becomes our conference room. Have you stopped to think how you come across in your online interactions?

Email, don't text. We get it—you're a millennial; you text. But hiring managers are often Baby Boomers and Gen Xers who communicate primarily by email. So because they are hiring you, you need to use the technology they are most comfortable with. In general, email is still considered the universal language for interpersonal business communications.

Check your online etiquette when writing email. Consider how you speak to others in person. Are you bubbly and gregarious? Are you subdued and practical? You don't have to become someone you're not. But to build solid relationships in the online space, don't risk sounding rude just because you're an introvert, busy, or distracted.

- **Greetings and closings**: Trust, once broken, is not easily repaired. And trust can be lost because of a hastily written email. Make sure you use a warm greeting and close with a salutation (unless a more casual relationship has already been established). It's kind. It shows thoughtfulness and care, and it helps avoid an unintended tone of disinterest, dismissal, or rudeness.

- **Content**: When writing the body of the email, remember that tone, volume, and nonverbal cues are hard to convey digitally. Punctuation and emoticons (smiley faces) can help to convey tone and meaning, but a carefully written email will do the same. The use of emoticons in professional communication is still up for debate. "If You're Happy and You Know It, Must I Know, Too?" asks *The New York Times* in an article on business emails. It's up to you to decide whether to use a smiley face in business communications, but regardless of emoticons, stop and review what you've written one last time before hitting "Send." If the content or tone could possibly be misconstrued, consider rewriting, picking up the phone, or walking over to a desk to try to prevent an avoidable miscommunication.

- **"Reply All"**: You received forty emails while you were out at lunch, of which only three are directly relevant to you and your work on a project. Enough said. Think before you hit "Reply All" and you'll save someone else the pain of an overstuffed inbox. You'll also earn their eternal gratitude.

Remember, technology is changing how we interact. Technology not only is altering the way we live our lives, but is even affecting the development of our brains. If we aren't conscious of how that affects our interactions with one another, our personal connections and relationships are likely to suffer.

Sherry Turkle, director of the MIT Initiative on Technology and Self and author of *Alone Together: Why We Expect More from Technology and Less from Each Other*, made this comment in *The Hedgehog Review* (Spring 2012): "We're moving from conversation to connection. In conversation we're present to each other in very powerful ways. Conversation is a kind of communication in which we're alive to each other, empathetic with each other, listening to each other. When we substitute Twitter or status updates on Facebook for this, we're losing something important."

With these wise words in mind, remember to make it your goal to both converse *and* connect in your communications with others.

Dig deeper!

For links to some of the topics covered in this chapter (including ways to optimize your use of LinkedIn, must-follow Twitter hashtags, emoticons and business communications, and the Belmont Goats, among many others), go to www.macslist.org/references.

3 Networking and Conducting Informational Interviews

Help other people help you!

On late August evenings, large crowds gather in Wallace Park in Northwest Portland to watch the Vaux's swifts roost in the chimney of Chapman Elementary School. This amazing natural event occurs only at this time of year, when thousands of swifts congregate in Portland to prepare for their annual migration to Central America and Venezuela. Each night, the spectacle begins as the swifts slowly start to communicate with each other and swirl into a pattern. As the spirals become denser and denser, the flock suddenly achieves critical mass. All at once the decision is made and thousands of birds fly into the chimney within a matter of minutes.

Just like the Vaux's swifts, you need to work with others to form a bigger "flock." Follow this rule of the four Cs: connect with others, communicate your ideas, and create community as part of your job search. You can't do it alone! Use your connections to form relationships and get to know people who may recommend you for a job. And remember–going to networking events also shows that you're active in your community and that you're willing to go the extra mile to find the right job.

Here's why you should network.

Some people are born networkers, others acquire networking skills, and still others have networking events thrust upon them. No matter which group you're in, you need to embrace the fact that networking and informational interviews are crucial tools in your job search. They get results.

The "hidden job market" is not a myth. Some estimates put the number of unadvertised jobs as high as eighty percent. Talk to hiring managers, human resource directors, and career counselors. They will tell you that most openings never appear on a job board. Positions go unadvertised because employers hire people they know or who come recommended by people they trust.

Applying online isn't enough. You can't rely just on responding to the openings you see on Mac's List and other job boards. If all you do is answer job ads, you will find yourself competing with dozens or even hundreds of other applicants. And those are tough odds, no matter how qualified you may be. If you want to be in the mix, you need to make standard networking techniques like informational interviewing, involvement in professional groups, and staying in touch with former colleagues a regular part of your professional routine.

It's a great way to hone your people skills. Networking is hard work. Like any skill, it takes time, patience, and a lot of practice. You will also experience rejection. People may ignore you at a social event, fail to answer your emails, or not return your telephone calls. But here's the good news: you have the most important asset every networker needs—a group of friends, family members, classmates, and current and past coworkers. And with enough education and effort, you can master even the most advanced networking skills.

It will energize your job search. No matter how hard it may be to reach out to others while you're looking for work, talking to others is rewarding. It can also be inspiring, interesting, informative, and just plain fun. Keep reminding yourself — going out to talk to other people who share your interests and passions definitely beats staying home and binge watching episodes of *RuPaul's Drag Race* while polishing off a pint of Salt & Straw ice cream.

Advice From an In The Know Portland Expert

Networking Schmetworking:
Tips for Genuine Connection in Oregon

by **Jen Violi**   Mentor, Editor, Facilitator, and Author of
Putting Makeup on Dead People

Even the words "networking event" make me queasy—forcing a smile, talking about what I "do," engaging in conversations that make me feel like I'm on trial or a contestant on *The Dating Game*. But beneath the sticky schmooze layer, neworking means connecting, an action I happen to love. And connection is essential when you're job hunting—a taxing endeavor, here in Portland or anywhere.

Often, traditional networking events can feed the stress, and connections can feel anxious, awkward, or needy—exactly like a bad date. The truth is, connection works best when there's ease. It doesn't have to be painful. At its heart, to network is to follow your natural inclinations toward connection.

Instead of going to a "networking event," consider where your people are. If, like me, your people are writers or word lovers, put yourself among them. Go to the upcoming meeting of Willamette Writers at The Old Church or to a reading at Powell's Books. Strike up a conversation. The common subject matter is built into the event; no need to force it.

For example, I love parties with activities. I've had several fiestas where I invite guests to make a Play-Doh birthday village, and I'm amazed at how much tangible tasks put us at ease. A shared activity lifts the pressure to force conversation. Suddenly, you have to ask someone to pass the blue and to let them know your Smurf is going to need a toadstool cottage.

When I first moved to Portland, I knew I needed to find work and to meet people. I was alone in a new city, healing from a painful divorce and reeling from the loss of a writing gig. I was in no state to go to a networking event. I would have wept into the pretzels. Instead, I addressed my need to get grounded and stay sane through genuine connection.

Following my yearning to connect with others who valued the healing power of words, I started volunteering for Write Around Portland. Through one of the writing workshops, I met a spitfire of a woman who, when the workshop ended, invited me to her birthday party, through which I met another woman writer who is now one of my regular clients.

That's just one example of dozens, all built on instances of me following my natural inclinations. Networking—in the most painless way possible.

So consider yourself encouraged to put yourself in situations you love, with people who care about the things you care about, and let those connections happen.

Work the room like a pro.

Networking is all about making connections, and your goal is to make as many *meaningful* contacts as possible at each event you attend. Follow these rules and you'll be the master of your own networking universe.

Prepare yourself. Set yourself up for success before you even set foot in the door.

- **Polish up your LinkedIn profile.** Upload a professional-looking headshot, update all of your information, and fill in the "Summary" section in a way that promotes who you are and what you do well. Finally, create a custom public profile URL.

- **Make a business card.** Handing out a card at an event boosts your chances of cultivating a relationship after the drinks are over. Make sure it includes your contact information and the URL to your LinkedIn profile. Create a title for yourself (graduate student, strategic communicator, social media evangelist) that helps people remember who you are or what you want to do.

- **Check the privacy settings for all of your social media platforms.** Make sure your virtual self is looking good and not unprofessional. You'll want to avoid any potential employer having the opportunity to see your photos from a rowdy Fourth of July barbecue.

- **Know your story in advance.** Have a thirty-second introduction ready that explains who you are and what your job goals are. Make eye contact and have a firm handshake ready. Wear casual business attire but include creative touches, such as an interesting accessory that may help break the ice.

- **Set goals. Know what you want to accomplish.** Have a clear idea of what you intend to gain before you arrive. Possible goals might include meeting potential employers, connecting with other job seekers for advice and support, reconnecting with current contacts and former colleagues, or identifying areas of interest or inquiry that you want to explore further.

- **Manage expectations. Begin by knowing what you want.** You don't have to walk away with a job offer for an event to be a success. Focus on building and maintaining relationships.

Don't be shy—dive right in. Once you're at the event, take a deep breath and get off to a good start by doing the following.

- **Arrive early.** The early bird catches the connections. Settle in, breathe deeply, and you'll be better company and enjoy yourself more. Don't be the person who arrives late.

- **Stand by the food or drinks.** It's easy to strike up a brief, one-on-one conversation in the buffet line or at a snack table. It's also a setting that gives you a few minutes with one person and the ability to move on if you wish.

- **Put the name tag on right.** Right-handed people instinctively put a name tag on their left side. Big mistake. To make your name tag easy to see, put it on your right, something only 10% of us do.

- **Repeat names.** Restate the name of the person you're meeting. ("Nice to meet you, Eric. I'm Mac.") This helps you remember. Don't worry about the repetition. As Dale Carnegie said, "Names are the *sweetest* and most important *sound in any language.*" (See the end-of-chapter resource list for ten tips for remembering names.)

- **Ditch people you already know.** It's tempting to stick with people you see frequently. Instead, strike out on your own. Remember, you're there to grow your network.

- **Approach others.** See someone standing alone? They will be secretly relieved when you walk up, introduce yourself, and start a conversation. Not sure about joining a small group? Look for friendly body language and casual conversation, good signals they are open to talking with others.

- **Know what to say and what you want.** Come with a few stories to share that have nothing to do with work. Talk about a new movie you like, your vacation plans, or a restaurant you want to try. But be selfish, too. Is there a connection you want to make, an introduction you'd like to arrange? Have your anecdotes and asks ready before you enter the room.

- **Be memorable.** The more "important" a person is, the more people he or she will meet at a networking event. If you want the person to remember you, find a way to make a personal connection so that you will stand out.

- **Ask questions and then listen to the answers.** The really smart people at a networking event don't talk and talk and talk, especially about themselves. They ask great questions. This puts others at ease. Open-ended questions work best. Ask about someone's involvement in the sponsoring organization, their connection to the host, or the distance they've traveled. You'll also hear great stories and get important insights. Knowing how to listen is one of the most valuable skills of all.

- **Be a host**. Make introductions and invite others to join a group. People will be grateful and remember your kindness.

- **Do good turns for others.** Does a conversation reveal common interests and make you think of websites, articles, or other helpful material? Offer to pass along this information. This allows you to be a resource after you return to the office and gives a legitimate reason to exchange business cards.

- **Remember: quality beats quantity**. Don't be that person who collects a stack of business cards as though they were rare baseball cards. Instead, talk to a few people with the goal of building real relationships.

- **Take notes**. After you leave an event, take a moment to jot a few facts on the back of the cards of people you've met. Reference that information in a followup note. Don't rely on your memory.

- **Meet on LinkedIn**. Did you have a good conversation with someone? Send a LinkedIn invitation to remain connected. Avoid the standard text and write a personal note.

- **Stay connected. Follow up**. Consider asking for—or giving—an informational interview. This could be a formal meeting in an office, a quick cup of coffee, or a lunch. If you're attending a regular lunch or event sponsored by a professional group, look for people you've met before.

Look for opportunities to network.

OK! You're convinced you need to network and you've just learned how to do it, but where do you begin? How do you find places to practice your new skills?

Tap into your existing social and professional networks. Check out professional association meetings, conferences, or other events. Whether you volunteer or simply show up, you'll make important contacts and good friends. And by learning about the latest developments, you'll make yourself more valuable to your current (and future) employer. But don't stop there. Let everyone know you are looking for work—family, friends, classmates, alumni, and colleagues.

Make use of all of LinkedIn's potential. Most of us have a basic LinkedIn profile but don't take advantage of all the platform's capabilities. What you might not know is that LinkedIn is a *great* tool for building a network! It is easy to use— just get in there and connect with everyone you know or meet. Send them a personal note, follow up, schedule coffee with the ones you really like, keep in touch, and cultivate your network for job security, professional support, and opportunities you never even imagined.

Attend a career fair. These events can be very useful for meeting potential employers and learning about entry-level jobs and student internships. They also provide a perfect opportunity to practice and sharpen job interview skills.

Just remember to plan ahead by creating a thirty-second introduction that explains who you are and what job goals you have. Have questions ready for the people you want to meet. Avoid general queries such as, "Tell me about your company." Instead, ask about topics that demonstrate you researched the employer and are thinking about the firm's needs. Then, if you learn that an employer is hiring, ask about next steps in the process. Bring pen and paper or a smartphone to take notes and make an appointment if appropriate. Finally, make it easy for others to find you. Bring resumes and business cards so that employers can follow up with you after the event.

Go to organized networking events. Target networking events that reflect your career and professional interests. With so many events around town, it's easy to find ones that speak directly to your needs. Although nowhere near a comprehensive list, here are twenty-five that the Mac's List staff likes. (See the end-of-chapter resource list for links to these events.)

- **For Portland professionals in general:**

  Calagator: This is a unified calendar of events specific to the technology community of Portland. (There are too many events to list here!)

  Green Drinks Portland: This environmentally conscious group meets every first Tuesday of the month at the beautiful Ecotrust building in the Pearl District.

  The Nonprofit Association of Oregon: This statewide network of nonprofit professionals and organizations maintains a comprehensive list of events and workshops.

  The Nonprofit Network: This group organizes an excellent annual conference and frequent events for nonprofit professionals in southwestern Washington state and the Portland area.

Oregon Entrepreneurs Network: This is the largest entrepreneur assistance organization in the state of Oregon.

Portland Business Alliance Emerging Professionals of Portland (EPOP): Connecting emerging civic and business leaders to those who are established in the Portland community, this group hosts not only networking events but outdoor excursions, too!

Portland Toastmasters: Improve your public speaking through local club meetings, training seminars, and speech contests. A typical group is made up of twenty to thirty people and meets weekly.

PRSA PDX New Pros: Follow this local Public Relations Society of America group on Twitter for the latest information in events, jobs, and relevant news from members.

Say Hey: Partners in Diversity puts on quite a party at this quarterly event aimed at connecting the multicultural community. Highly recommended for all young professionals.

Schmooze: Created by Harlo Interactive, this nonprofit event happens six times per year. No RSVP, no fee, and no name tags, this event is all about connecting people.

SEMpdx: Creator of the very popular SEMpdx Rooftop Networking Party, this group knows how to create buzz. If you missed this year's event, make sure to put it on your calendar for next time.

Society for Marketing Professional Services of Oregon: Its mission is to advocate for, educate, and connect leaders in the building industry.

Social Media Club PDX: This local networking club aims to expand media literacy, share lessons learned, encourage industry standards, and promote ethics in social media.

- **For women:**

  Hub Dot: At Hub Dot events, attendees use colored dots instead of name tags as a way to help women start conversations and make connections in an authentic way. Hub Dot is about the cross-pollination of ideas, talent, support, and friendships.

  The Link: This community of female professionals in Portland promises to connect you with other accomplished women in the area.

Portland Female Executives: PDXfx holds monthly events for Portland female executives in various venues.

Women's Center for Leadership: This great group of women has a local executive female speaker once a month, meeting at a local bar.

Women in Insurance and Financial Services: For those women in the finance industry, this is the place to network with women in your profession.

Young Women Social Entrepreneurs: One recent event focused on women entrepreneurs in the Portland Craft Beer Scene. Follow them on Facebook for the latest events and information for members.

- **For communications professionals:**

AMA-PDX (American Marketing Association): If you can break away for a long lunch, the Portland chapter of The American Marketing Association puts on two luncheons per month, each offering an informative presentation. Even if you don't work in marketing, AMA events are relevant to all communications professionals.

Healthcare Communicators of Oregon: Committed to helping healthcare professionals in the communications fields grow professionally and connect with others in their field, this organization holds conferences throughout the year.

International Association of Business Communicators: Each month this organization holds luncheon events with a guest speaker presenting on a topic relevant to the communications industry. Its events are a great place to gain deeper understanding of interesting topics and also a good venue to meet like-minded people and exchange information.

Portland Advertising Federation: PAF really taps into the creative side of the communications sector in Portland. Its events are a great place to mingle with professionals from all sorts of organizations, from advertising agencies to design firms.

The Portland New Generations Rotary Club: Committed to building a community of professionals dedicated to service and global citizenship, this organization holds many events throughout the month.

PRSA-PDX (Public Relations Society of America): The PRSA is not to be forgotten on this list for communicators of all ages. Many influential leaders attend their meetings and organized events.

Request informational interviews strategically.

Now that you're putting yourself out there, you're probably making some great contacts and coming across some interesting leads to follow. Congratulations! You're ready to take the next step—asking people to give you an informational interview.

But before you start inviting people out for coffee, learn how informational interviews work and how you can use them to target specific job-hunting goals.

Start with friends and family. Turn to the people who know you best: your family and friends. Don't neglect to tell your kid sister, your neighbors, or your friends in the kickball league about your job goals and whom you want to meet.

Work your LinkedIn page. As mentioned previously, an up-to-date LinkedIn profile is vital to the success of any job search. One of the biggest advantages of staying in touch with former colleagues and fellow students on LinkedIn: you can see their networks and where they reach. Don't be shy. Ask for an introduction if you see a connection you want to make.

Know the players. Reach out to the leaders of your occupation's professional association. Also look at published guides of leading employers, like the *Portland Business Journal's* indispensable *Book of Lists* (free at the Multnomah County Central Library) and *Oregon Business* magazine's "100 Best Companies" and "100 Best Nonprofits," as well as *The Oregonian's* "People on the Move" column. (See links to these in the end-of-chapter resources list.)

Don't forget your alma mater. Many universities have an online database of graduates, often leaders in their professions, who have offered to talk to fellow alumni about job hunting. Have you visited your school's alumni database? If not, you'll be amazed at the people who are willing to see you.

Do the following when you're ready to make contact. So how do you set up the meeting? Here are guidelines to follow when asking for an informational interview, along with a sample request email. (Want to learn more about scheduling informational interviews? The Career Center at Chemeketa Community College has a number of resources, including a sample letter for asking for an appointment. The career services office at Reed College also has very good online resources on these topics. See end-of-chapter resource list.)

- **Say who sent you.** People are more likely to make time if you are introduced by someone they know, so mention your common connection.

- **Describe what you want.** Want to learn more about an unfamiliar profession? Hoping to uncover upcoming job opportunities in the field? Want introductions to other leaders? Be specific and you make it easier for others to help you.

- **Share an agenda in advance.** Explain the purpose of the meeting and how you believe the person you want to see can help. Don't leave anything to the imagination. Someone is much more likely to agree to a meeting if you tell them in advance what you want.

- **Include your resume.** No, you're not applying for a job, but your resume provides an excellent summary of your background, and those you meet will welcome this information.

- **Set time limits.** A good informational interview requires no more than fifteen to thirty minutes. Let people know this is all the time you want.

- **Follow up.** Haven't heard back? Try following "the rule of three" with any scheduling request. Make three followup attempts—spaced four or five business days apart—before giving up.

- **Use this as a model.** Here's an example of an email you might send when requesting an informational interview.

> SUBJECT LINE: Request for Informational Interview/Writing at Suggestion of ‹contact›
>
> I am writing at the suggestion of ‹contact› at ‹business affiliation›. I am exploring opportunities in ‹career field› in Portland. As you can see from the attached resume, I've had considerable experience creating and leading successful ‹type of work› in Oregon and other states.
>
> ‹Contact› thought you would be good source of information about ‹career field› in Portland, upcoming jobs in the field, and other people I might contact. I'm hoping you might have fifteen to thirty minutes to meet with me in the next few weeks.
>
> Please let me know if this might be possible and what dates and times are most convenient for you. I look forward to hearing from you.
>
> Best regards,
>
> ‹your name›

Structure your interview carefully.

Plan ahead and show the person you're interviewing that you've spent time in advance—so that you don't waste his or hers. Follow these do's and don'ts to master the art of the informational interview.

Make sure you do this!

- **Read up in advance.** There's no excuse for not reading the company website and the LinkedIn profile of the person you're asking for help. Doing so gives you the information you need to make the most of the conversation and signals you want to use the time well.
- **Identify your goal.** Every informational interview must have a purpose. Your exact goals depend on your needs. These could include introducing yourself to leaders in your field, growing your professional network, and reconnecting with former colleagues. Be clear about what you want before you walk through the door.
- **Bring specific questions.** Come prepared with an "ask." Perhaps it's an introduction to someone at the company that interests you. Or it could be advice about how to handle challenges you face in switching careers. Whatever the request, be specific. Email the questions if that makes you more comfortable. Don't know what to ask? Here are some ideas:

  What educational background do you think is needed for the kind of work that you do?

  Are there any other organizations similar to yours that I should know about and research?

  Is there someone you think I should meet who might be helpful in my search for a career like yours?

  What associations do you recommend I join?

  Where should I volunteer in order to grow my skill set and meet people in my industry?

- **Leave early.** You never know if there will be traffic, if there will be parking, or if all the buildings will be identical so that you are running around like a crazy person trying to find the right one. Give yourself enough time so that you are waiting in the lobby ten minutes early. The person you are scheduled to meet with is doing you a favor, so do not waste his or her time.

- **Be polite to everyone**. Greet everyone, smile, make eye contact, and shake hands with everyone you meet. Start your interview by saying thank you to your interviewee for taking the time to meet with you.

- **Tell your story.** Remember when we advised you to work on a quick summary of your job-hunting journey? Now's the time to tell it. It will help your listener understand what you do so that they can suggest contacts or remember you when a job opening comes up.

- **Ask questions and listen carefully to the answers.** Never ask for information you can read on a company website or a LinkedIn profile. Doing so says you didn't prepare. Instead, ask your questions and listen or take notes while they are answered.

- **Wind down and wrap up.** With your last five minutes, finish the interview and summarize what decisions were made and what action steps you agreed upon. Make a brief, positive goodbye and—above all—express your gratitude.

- **Ask how you can help them.** People who request informational interviews always stand out when they finish by asking what they can do for the interviewee. Don't forget that you have much to offer to others no matter what your stage of career.

- **Buy the coffee.** No one expects to be rewarded for giving an informational interview, but it's nice if the coffee is on the person making the request.

Don't make these mistakes!

- **Arrive too early.** Leave home early and try to arrive ten minutes before your interivew, but don't go to the person's office more than five minutes before the appointed time. He or she has other business. Instead, take a walk around the block or catch up on your email at a coffee shop.

- **Dress down.** Offices are much less formal these days. Business casual works most of the time. Always know the office culture, however, and avoid being *too* casual. You definitely do *not* want to show up in a sweat-soaked Spandex cycling jersey and shorts.

- **Forget your resume or business card.** Always offer to share your resume at the start of the meeting even when you've emailed it in advance. The person you're seeing will be grateful to review your resume again and refresh his or her memory about your background. Don't forget to exchange cards at the beginning or end of the meeting and use the information to stay in touch with your contact on LinkedIn.

- **Have no ask.** An unsuccessful meeting is one that ends without any next steps identified. Perhaps you want insights in changing careers, advice on how managers in your field hire, or introductions to new contacts. Have your list ready. The people you're meeting wouldn't see you if they didn't want to help.
- **Ask for a job.** Never ask for a job in an informational interview. You're there to network, not to apply for a position.
- **Assume unlimited time.** Your time is your most valuable asset. The same is true for the person you're meeting. You specified a certain amount of time in your request for the interview. Now stick to it. Bring the meeting to a close on schedule.

Don't drop the ball!

If you follow the steps above, you're ready to rock the informational interview. But after the interview don't forget to do one last thing—follow up!

Send a thank-you note. Handwritten notes are nice. Email is just fine. Whatever the format, just do it and do so within twenty-four hours. People are busy, and while they may be willing to do informational interviews, you want to make sure that their generosity does not go unnoticed. People will notice (and remember) if you don't thank them. And while you're at it, why not include a gift card for a cup of coffee in your thank-you note? You will create terrific good will.

In the thank-you note, feel free to politely remind the interviewee of what he or she agreed to do. Examples are, "Thank you for offering to connect me with X," or "Thank you for offering to send me information about that volunteer opportunity with Y."

Connect via social media. Invite the people you meet to connect with you on LinkedIn. Look for ways to stay in touch, such as interacting with them on Twitter, Instagram, and Google+, or leaving comments on their blog or LinkedIn posts.

Stay in touch. Look for ways to remain in contact, such as forwarding relevant articles or links, sharing news about mutual contacts, or letting people know when you've found work. Don't neglect your network! Your career will be better for it.

Burn no bridges! Every city, no matter how large, is really a small town. This is definitely true of Portland, where the local joke is that here there are only two or three degrees of separation. Over the course of a career, you will keep meeting the same people. Always treat others with the same respect and courtesy you expect. You never know who may be sitting on a hiring panel or reviewing a contract proposal.

Dig deeper!

For links to some of the topics covered in this chapter (including the hidden job market, more networking tips, numerous networking events, and the Vaux's swifts at Chapman Elementary school, among many others), go to www.macslist.org/references.

4 Looking for Opportunities and Experience

Start moving toward your goals!

This is a town where people love to dress up and try out different roles. From SantaCon (which originated here) to our enthusiastic local celebration of Talk Like a Pirate Day, it doesn't take much of an excuse for Portlanders to throw on a costume and take to the streets. One such event is the Portland Zombie Walk, a family-friendly event that occurs each October. It began as a flash mob in 2006, and across the years it has expanded to include an official walking route and thousands of zombies. Recent celebrations have included bonus activities such as a "Thriller" dance and a "Walking Dead" viewing party.

Don't just lumber through your job search like a zombie! Be on the lookout for new opportunities to gain valuable work experience or skills, make formal connections with people who can give you advice and guidance, or locate specialized resources for job listings you might not otherwise encounter. If job hunting is getting you down, don't just roll over and play dead. Reanimate your search with new experiences, professional advice, and ideas!

Be an intern.

Whether you are a recent college grad looking for your first job or someone looking to change careers and transition into a new one, you need to get some pertinent job experience under your belt. The good news is that there are opportunities all around you—just keep your eyes open and find ways to take advantage of them.

Internships are a great way to boost your resume and ease your transition into the workforce, for those just starting out and for those returning after a hiatus as well. Sure, the Portland job market is tough, but according to the *Portland Business*

Journal, one upside of our tight job market is that it has increased the number of available local internships.

Whether your internship is paid or offered through an academic program, just make sure that it is a good opportunity for you to acquire the skills and information you need for your chosen field. Here are ten tips for maximizing the value of your internship. (The Career Services Office at George Fox University also has good ideas about how to make the most of the intern experience. See end-of-chapter resources.)

Don't let the hierarchy scare you. It can be nerve-racking working around successful people, but don't be afraid of them. Just because someone is a "higher-up" doesn't mean that he or she won't give you the time of day. Always recognize that people are busy and their time is limited. But use your new colleagues as a resource to help you learn more about the industry or how to start planning your next step. Your coworkers are just people when you strip away the job title.

Be efficient. Look for ways to do your repetitive assignments as quickly as possible. For instance, instead of sharing documents through Dropbox, set up a live document on Google Docs. Before implementing any new method, ask for approval. Even if your bosses say no, they will appreciate your initiative.

Make deadlines. In high school, deadlines were forgiving. In college, they were firm enough. But in the real world, people really, really like work to be done on time. When you are late, you are likely messing with someone's bottom line, and most people generally don't enjoy that—at all.

Ask for new projects. If you are completing your work in a timely manner, talk to your supervisor about taking on an extra project. Perhaps there is a client you are interested in working with or you want to shadow one of your firm's staff for a day.

Ask questions. Everyone fears sounding foolish in front of an office of smart people. In some cases it may be bad not to know, but it's always worse not to ask the question. Besides, learning more was the impetus for taking an internship in the first place, right?

Switch up your routine. Vary your media intake every day. Read a different newspaper or book, watch a different news program, or rent an old movie that made a cultural impact a few decades ago. Do anything to learn something new so that you can relate to different perspectives.

Make connections. By the middle of an internship, you have proven that you are intelligent and hardworking. Now is the time to begin developing relationships with your office colleagues. Make an effort to talk with everyone in your office and connect on LinkedIn. Each person at your company is an ideal candidate for an informational interview.

Stay on top of current trends. Be well-rounded in your cultural references. There is nothing worse than a room full of people understanding a reference and you're standing in the corner scratching your head in bewilderment. Try to buff up your knowledge of popular culture—not just current, but over the last couple of decades. It never hurts to be well-rounded.

That said, be yourself. In a job climate where culture fit has become the X factor in a hiring decision, it pays not to be a drone. Indeed, there is nothing wrong with sticking out for being a little different. Better to enjoy your surroundings than to try to keep up a façade for your whole career.

But don't be your harshest critic. It's easy to obsess over what we think of as a wrong decision. Strive to do the best you can, but know that you are human and mistakes are inevitable. Take your internship seriously, but don't be too hard on yourself if something goes wrong. Apologize, take responsibility for your mistake, and use it as a learning experience.

Advice From an In The Know Portland Expert

There's No Place for Fire Dancing During Your Internship
(and Other Tips for Being a Great Intern).

by **Jennie Day-Burget** Former Vice President and Managing Director, Prichard Communications

I supervised many interns at Prichard Communications. While their backgrounds, hairstyles, and majors have varied, they all had one thing in common—limited experience in a professional environment. I don't fault them for this—most have been young, bright, and aspiring professionals who haven't had much opportunity to get professional experience yet—and that's where I can help.

Check your email! We don't assign email addresses as a matter of ritual—we assign them because that's how we talk to you. There is an expectation in the business world that if I email you, you'll email me back with the information I seek in a timely fashion.

Dress for the job. We're pretty business casual around here, but by any definition of "business casual," Portlanders' favorite furry winter boots and zip-up hoodies are not appropriate. Excessive cleavage makes people feel awkward, and too much perfume might kill us all. Ripped concert t-shirts really don't inspire me to think of you as someone I can turn to with a pressing request. Shorts? If I'd see it at a cabana, I probably shouldn't see it in the office.

Replace casual vernacular with professional vernacular. You're no longer conversing with your peers; you're conversing with business professionals. Adjust your language accordingly. Replace "Hey Jennie, there's a guy up front here to see you" with "Jennie, there's a gentleman up here asking for you." See the difference? By using professional language, you've proven yourself a professional and also made our office look professional. And I will like you for that.

Believe in yourself because I believe in you. I didn't hire you just to hire someone. I hired you because I believe you can do a job for me. Don't shy away from assignments because you worry you can't do them. You can, or you wouldn't have gotten the internship.

Your success (or not) will follow you well beyond your internship. Come in smelling like you partied your pants off at the Dante's fire dancer show last night? Leave the Dante's at Dante's. There's just no place for fire dancing on our (current) client roster. And workplace booze events like this will follow you … I promise.

Use your inside voice. I know, I know. It sounds like I'm talking to a third grader, but seriously, USE YOUR INSIDE VOICE! It's hard to concentrate when the interns parked outside of your office are recounting last weekend's kegger. I don't want to hear about it, so save that conversation for the bus.

Volunteer.

As part of your job search you should always look for opportunities to connect with like-minded people. One way to accomplish this is by volunteering. Doing so opens doors and will give you new ideas as well as concrete experience and skills. Here are five reasons that volunteering as part of your job hunt in Portland is time well spent.

It expands your network. Volunteering can open many doors to opportunities you may never have thought of and allow you to meet people outside your comfort zone. This may be just the ticket to learning about that quiet startup or a cutting-edge master's program. New connections might even steer you down a path to a great fellowship or consulting gig, exposing you to ideas and opportunities that you never even knew existed.

It boosts your morale. It's no secret that giving to the world around us makes us feel good. The job search can be hard. So volunteer your time and improve your perspective. It might just give you the boost of energy you needed to get through the week.

It improves your resume. So you say that caring for the environment is your passion? Employers look to your resume as proof that your actions really do align with your beliefs. They want to see that you donate your spare time to the cause you care about and that you are committed to your ideals. Volunteer positions on your resume show that you are a well-rounded individual eager to make a difference.

It lets you test out a career or new sector. Thinking of leaving your job in communications to become a midwife? Volunteer in a hospital or women's clinic before you take the plunge! You may save yourself countless hours in the classroom and lost money if you experience the industry first as a volunteer.

It lets you practice your skills or learn new ones. Are you a master at digital strategy? Volunteer your expertise with a nonprofit organization and you can build your resume and references. Thinking of quitting your day job to become a writer? Offer to create press releases or be a contributing blogger for your favorite nonprofit. You'll gain valuable experience and insight into the field.

To get started, check out the Nonprofit Association of Oregon's Volunteer Toolkit and then search the National Center for Charitable Statistics (NCCS) for an organization you are interested in volunteering with. (See end-of-chapter resources.)

Try summer (or other temporary) employment.

Having a temporary summer job lets you get valuable and transferable skills without making a long-term commitment to a particular profession. Summer jobs allow workers to explore the working world and learn something unique in the process.

The benefits don't apply only to students. From a business standpoint, a multitude of positive outcomes can result from creating summer jobs. Summer workers offer a cost-effective way to increase an organization's productivity and also give staff members an opportunity to gain supervisory experience.

Advice From an In The Know Portland Expert

Hello College Students, I'm Talking to You!

by **Gabrielle Nygaard** Fulbright Scholar, Linfield College graduate, and former Prichard Communications intern

The question every college senior dreads but can't avoid: *What are you going to do after graduation?* Don't despair—I have two answers for you!

Don't wait until you graduate to take action. Venture out of the bubble that insulates life at every university and into the real world *now*. Put yourself out there. Invest some time off campus. Activities and accomplishments outside of your institution will serve you well for many reasons. Not only will "real world" experience hone your practical skills and provide professional connections, but it will also enhance your resume.

Employers want to see diverse experience and that you have what it takes to succeed in a professional field outside student employment, student programs, and other school-sponsored endeavors. Try an internship or volunteer position off campus. Classwork can be a good way to display your skills, but published or paid work samples will make your portfolio shine. As my friend—a recent graduate who snagged a marketing job in Oregon wine country—forewarned me, outside of the school setting there are no course syllabi, assignment rubrics, and due dates to guide our work. The sooner we experience and adapt to the flow of "real" work, the better.

Consider the benefits of a bridge year. Traveling, interning, volunteering, or otherwise wandering the world will help you learn about yourself. Cultural and service experiences are the classic setups for stepping out of your comfort zone. A key to finding your career niche is knowing thyself. By expanding your horizons you can explore and challenge yourself. Whether domestic or abroad, a bridge year can expose you to new ways of thinking and vast opportunities.

A bridge year is also a chance to identify and hone your personal strengths, as well as to try your hand at developing new skills. What you find about your likes, dislikes, and abilities may reinvigorate or realign your career goals—and the knowledge you gain can help you reach them. And, by getting out of your normal sphere, you'll make all kinds of connections and new allies, both personal and professional. Not only will the experience shape you as a person, it will add something special to help yours stand out in a sea of resumes.

Find a mentor.

Let's face it; sometimes we all need a little push to help set us back on track, or to help us recognize opportunities that may be staring us in the face while we're looking the other way. Finding a mentor and then setting up monthly meetings can help you reevaluate your goals and keep you from losing hope. It's also a great opportunity to receive constructive criticism from a professional in your field.

Here are three reasons it is important to have a mentor and three tips for identifying a mentor in your network.

Why do I need a mentor?

- **Professional development:** A mentor can help you identify your long-term goals and the strategies to help you achieve them. Each time you meet, you can discuss progress and obstacles and set goals for the future.
- **Professional support:** Mentors can keep you going and point out opportunities you may have missed. They can also help you with your resume and lead you to key resources.

- **Creative thinking:** Brainstorming with someone who isn't mired in your specific challenges often produces great ideas. Struggling with how to find internships or volunteer opportunities? Check in with your mentor to identify new areas to research.

How do I find a mentor?

- **Identify someone.** Look at your network of people. Whom do you admire the most and why? Does this person do something well that you'd like to learn about? Is he or she an expert in an area where you are looking to grow? Many professional organizations—such as the Portland chapter of the Public Relations Society of America, to cite just one example—also offer mentorship programs and networks.
- **Know your strengths and weaknesses.** In identifying a mentor, understand your own needs. Are you exploring work in new sectors? Starting your own business? Looking for ways to grow professionally? Find a person who has been there and can help you navigate the challenges.
- **Ask.** Many people agree to be a mentor purely for the sense of satisfaction in paying it forward. Start by simply asking for advice on one action or problem and then continue the relationship by showing them how they can help you.

Know where to find local job listings.

When looking for work, you can't rely on one source alone to learn about publicly advertised jobs. You need to dig deep. Local job search boards are a terrific way to find openings that may never appear on the big national job sites.

(And oh hey, by the way, did we mention that Mac's List is Portland's top source for jobs in the city and throughout Oregon at large? We did? OK, let's move on then...)

Here are some of the specialized job boards, lists, and blogs that we find particularly helpful. (See the end-of-chapter resource list.)

Public relations

- **Healthcare Communicators of Oregon:** This professional organization's volunteer-run job board is updated every quarter. Elsewhere on the site you can find information about conferences and other events the organization offers.

- **The Oregon Chapter of the International Association of Business Communicators (OIABC):** The website includes a job bank for communications professionals. Postings come from members who work in southwestern Washington and throughout Oregon.

- **PDXMindshare:** This site, which started as a forum for networking, has now evolved to include job postings from many local public relations companies. The website also includes a good blog, calendar, and information about the monthly networking events.

- **Portland Creative List:** You can always find public relations and communications jobs in this well-designed and organized site. There's also an excellent directory of local public relations firms and a calendar of industry events.

- **Portland Metro Chapter of the Public Relations Society of America (PRSA):** The new, simpler format of this organization's recently relaunched website includes a beefed-up job center that is regularly updated. You should also visit the job page of PRSA's Oregon Capital Chapter in Salem and the job page of PRSA's Greater Oregon Chapter in Eugene.

- **The School of Journalism and Communication at the University of Oregon:** The school's website includes public relations positions in its jobs database. Many of the opportunities are from across the country, but you can easily sort all listings by state.

Fundraising and development

- **The Chronicle of Philanthropy:** This is a national publication, of course, but its job section usually includes a small number of Oregon development and fundraising positions. You can sort listings by state and sector.

- **The Oregon and Southwest Washington Chapter of the Association of Fundraising Professionals:** The local AFP chapter's public page includes an RSS feed you can use to receive updates as new listings are added. Job postings are also included in the chapter's twice-monthly membership newsletter.

- **The Willamette Valley Development Officers (WVDO):** This professional organization has operated its excellent Job Source since 2005. You need to join WVDO in order to view the full job list.

"Green" jobs

- **EcoEmploy:** Since 1998, David Brierley has published EcoEmploy.com, which features jobs from all fifty states, including Oregon. The site has a resource section for Oregon that contains links to job pages of many environmental nonprofits, public agencies, and businesses.

- **Leonard Adler's Green Jobs Network:** This site has an Oregon page that includes separate sections for solar, wind, and LEED jobs.

- **MES Weekly:** There are normally hundreds of jobs, internships, and events for the Portland area on this blog published by the Masters in Environmental Studies (MES) program at the Evergreen State College in Olympia, Washington. Don't want to check the blog every day? You can sign up for a weekly newsletter or use the RSS feed. Under "Helpful Links" you'll also find a list of recommended job sites.

- **Portland Green Drinks: Managed by Voice for Oregon Innovation and Sustainability (VOIS),** Portland Green Drinks sponsors a well-attended monthly networking event. Its website includes a job board.

- **Sustainable Business Oregon:** Operated by the *Portland Business Journal*, the Sustainable Business Oregon's job board typically has several dozen listings.

Oregon film and television industry

- **Extras Only:** Want to be on *Portlandia* or *Grimm*? This private company is looking for people for both shows and also regularly casts extras for other television programs and movies.

- **Laika Studios:** This animation house in Hillsboro is best known for its movies *Coraline*, *ParaNorman*, and *The Boxtrolls*, but it also produces commercials. The careers section of the Laika website lists open positions.

- **Oregon Film:** A useful resource from the East Portland–based Governor's Office of Film and Television that includes a job hotline and an excellent list of internship opportunities.

- **Regional Arts & Culture Council:** You can usually find a number of positions in film and television on the job board operated by this publicly funded nonprofit.

Nonprofits

- **Bridgestar Jobs:** Launched by the Bridgespan Group, a Boston-based consulting company that works with nonprofits, this national job site allows sorting of positions by state. Typically, there are only a handful of jobs for Oregon, but they are often gigs not seen elsewhere.

- **CNRG, the Community Nonprofit Resource Group:** Largely volunteer-run, this organization based in Southwest Portland publishes a daily digest of jobs, internships, and other opportunities with Oregon nonprofits for more than 10,000 subscribers. The CNRG website also has many useful resources for learning more about the state's nonprofit community.

- **Idealist:** Created in 1995, Idealist features jobs and volunteer opportunities around the globe. One of its offices is here in Portland. Idealist's easy-to-use search function allows you to sort listings by state. There are almost always several dozen good nonprofit jobs open in Oregon.

Additional sources for temporary employment, internships, and volunteer opportunities

The best place to check for temporary employment is any local university job board or career services office. You should also check out InternMatch.com, a national website based in San Francisco that features many paid summer jobs and internships, including dozens of positions in Oregon. Discover volunteer positions at Hands On Greater Portland.

The Oregon Education Association is a local union that represents educators working in pre-kindergarten through twelfth grade public schools and community colleges. The association provides online resources, a calendar of events, and volunteer opportunities.

Dig deeper!

For links to some of the topics covered in this chapter (including places to find mentors, volunteer toolkits, sources for job listings, fire dancing at Dante's, and Portland's Zombie Walk, among many others), go to www.macslist.org/references.

5 Applying for a Job

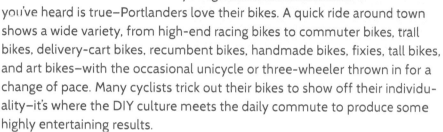

Show that you're one of a kind!

Every year Portland is ranked among the top most bike-friendly cities in the United States. Everything you've heard is true—Portlanders love their bikes. A quick ride around town shows a wide variety, from high-end racing bikes to commuter bikes, trail bikes, delivery-cart bikes, recumbent bikes, handmade bikes, fixies, tall bikes, and art bikes—with the occasional unicycle or three-wheeler thrown in for a change of pace. Many cyclists trick out their bikes to show off their individuality—it's where the DIY culture meets the daily commute to produce some highly entertaining results.

Let's face it—Portland is full of smart, creative, quirky, and talented people (just like you!). But because of that, you need to work harder to catch the eye of potential employers. So how do you take your job applications to new heights? C'mon—jump on your tall bike and let us be your guide along the route traveled by all the savvy Portland job applicants who've come before you.

Line up your references.

Before you start applying for jobs, make sure you've got your references primed and ready in advance. Handing a potential employer your references seems like a simple step in the application process, but it can be the most important key to getting an offer. A great reference can be your ticket to that new job, while a bad one can be the one thing that unwinds all of your hard work. Here's what you need to do before you give a potential employer your references.

Only put down great references. Don't list someone as a reference if he or she might only give you an average review. You need an advocate on your side, someone who will unequivocally support your future employment. If you're unsure, take that person off your reference list today or follow up beforehand to assure a stellar recommendation.

Make it easy. Get the updated contact information for your references and include the name, company, title, email address, and phone number. Also, note your relationship to this person—is he or she a past supervisor, employee, professor, or peer?

Give your references a heads up. To be a savvy job seeker, contact your references to let them know that they might receive a phone call or email from your potential employer. This gives your reference time to prepare and makes sure that he or she is ready to communicate and isn't caught off guard. And if you land an interview, reconnect afterwards to share what particular skills the employer is looking for in the ideal candidate.

Advice From an In The Know Portland Expert

How to Deal with a Bad Reference

by **Vicki Lind**, MS   Career Counselor and Marketing Coach

Marty was losing sleep. She'd done well in her job interview for a catalog proof-reader position, but she was anxious about her references. She couldn't stop imagining her ex-boss answering the reference call: "Marty? She's thorough, but slow. Really s-l-o-w."

If you're nervous about a recent employer's reference, relax. You're among good company. But right now, you need a strategy for damage control.

Does your past employer give references? Many employers only verify dates of employment and eligibility for rehire. Ask your former employer's human resource department about the references policy. If they don't give references, reacquaint yourself with a full night's sleep. If your past employer does give references, give plenty of other references to build a balanced picture. Include other people you've worked with: other bosses, members of the board, vendors, and so forth.

Avoid the negative if possible. If you're filling out an application and you are still employed in a negative situation, you'll likely have to provide the name of your current supervisor. Write "Please do not contact." The potential employer will assume that you do not want your supervisor to know that you plan to leave. This gives you more time to build a relationship with the prospective employer and emphasize your strengths.

Address the negative if it's not possible to avoid it. If you are no longer employed at the company, and you must list the supervisor's name who may criticize you, you have only two choices: include the name; or write "prefer to discuss in person." References are rarely contacted before the interview. The first impression you make can shape how a negative reference will be received later.

If asked, show integrity and honesty. Let's face it; we live in a connected world. Most hiring managers will ask their professional network about you, in addition to consulting your references. Assume that your prospective employer will find out about your conflicted relationship, so describe the conflict yourself without criticizing your ex-employer.

In Marty's case, she could position her strengths: "I pride myself on accuracy and a perfect final product in every printed piece. I may not be the fastest proof-reader, but I am very efficient; I never cause embarrassing mistakes or the need to reprint materials." She could back up her work with references from other former coworkers and positive references on LinkedIn.

By the time the reference call came around, Marty's interviewers were not surprised to hear her ex-supervisor's criticism for her slow pace. They did give her the job as proofreader, where she proofs hundreds of catalogs before printing thousands of flawless copies. And she sleeps very well.

Editor's Note: This text was written with help from Mike Russell of PivotalWriting.com.

Ace your application.

Sometimes landing a new job is a matter of luck. You don't know who might tell you about an unadvertised opening or how you will hit it off with a potential employer in an interview. What you can control is how you apply for a job. Here are some general do's and don'ts for acing the job application process.

Do ...

- **Target your applications.** The best cover letters and resumes discuss your skills and qualifications for a particular job. Whether you're applying for a government job or to a private employer, use keywords from the position description because both sectors rely on automated tracking systems to screen applications. Yes, it takes more time to do this, but it will put you ahead of those who email a generic set of application materials.

- **Include a cover letter.** A good cover letter written specifically for the job you want always stands out. Not sending a cover letter is a lost opportunity and signals a lack of interest on your part.

- **Show that you have the education and experience to make the employer's life easier.** For example, did you win an award for a social media campaign you produced? Tell an employer how that experience has prepared you to tackle the company's social media strategy.

- **Demonstrate that you did your research.** Don't email an application if you haven't looked at the hiring company or organization's website and you don't know what it is that they do.

- **Share your enthusiasm.** Nothing wins over potential employers like someone who shows excitement when talking about the job description. And don't just stop there. Say how excited you are to try something new!

Don't ...

- **Lie or misrepresent yourself.** Avoid fiction on your resume or elsewhere, be it hyperbole or straight-up fabrication. Find the most effective way to present your qualifications and skills, but make sure everything is solidly grounded in fact. You can fool some of the people all of the time, and all of... No, let's just stop right there. *It will catch up to you in the end*, so quit while you're ahead.

- **Make a typo.** Typographical errors are the fastest way to move your resume to the rejection pile. Catch typos—and mistakes in spelling, punctuation, and grammar—by reading your application aloud, a favorite tactic of famed writing coach William Zinsser. The ear is your best editor.

- **Ignore minimum qualifications.** No employer expects you to have every skill in a position announcement. But you need to meet the minimum qualifications, such as a college degree. Someone fresh out of college, for example, shouldn't apply for a job that asks for three years of professional experience.

- **Talk only about yourself.** Employers want to know how you can solve their problems. Yes, express your enthusiasm for the opportunity, but use your cover letter and an interview to show what you can do for a company and how you can make your new supervisor's life easier.
- **Gimmick up.** Avoid adding scent to your resume unless you're Reese Witherspoon in *Legally Blonde*. Don't tell jokes, make puns, or use sarcasm in a cover letter. Ditch the colored stationery and keep the design of your resume clear and simple.
- **Be too humble.** Humility is a good quality and shows discipline, but you have bragging rights when it comes to getting a job. Don't be afraid to let your hard work shine, be confident, and tell employers why you are the one who can make their life easier. Find the balance and wow them!

Create a great cover letter. According to Mara Woloshin (remember her from Chapter 2?), principal at Woloshin Communications, Inc. and frequent Mac's List blog contributor, job candidates often think of their cover letter as a last-minute item. Yet the letter that accompanies your resume has a very specific purpose. It is a demonstration of your knowledge of the organization and the position you are applying for. It is also a litmus test of your overall writing and communication skills.

A cover letter is a great vehicle for grabbing attention and holding it. Here are some tips for making the most of this opportunity when you apply for your next job.

- **Read up.** Research the company or organization's goals, mission, and history. Find out whether it has been in the news recently and, if so, why. Learn as much as you can about its background and current needs. And don't forget to include references to that information so that the reader knows you have done your homework.
- **Get personal.** If possible, find out the name of the decision maker and then address the cover letter directly to that person. Use a last name unless you have been introduced or referred by someone. In matters of etiquette, it's always better to err on the side of caution!
- **Be original.** Open with some kind of attention-grabbing statement or question that makes the reader want to learn more about you and your background.

- **Explain how you can solve problems.** Study the hiring company's social media accounts, read its blog posts, and show how your experience and skills will be an asset to the company. Explain your ideas here (and later on, in your interview).

- **Keep it active.** Stick to the point and use the active voice. When possible, use language from the company or organization's website or social media accounts. Try to imitate the style of its communications as much as possible.

- **Avoid repetition and trite language.** Don't summarize your resume, and don't fall back on formulaic expressions that contribute little to your message. Stay away from slang, jargon, or clichés. Keep things straightforward, direct, and simple.

- **Follow the rule of three for a short but dynamic cover letter.** Mara suggests having three key points and three sentences per paragraph. If your letter is longer than a page, you may be over-sharing or rambling.

- **Ask for the interview.** Always conclude with an ask. Request an interview and then follow up in a timely manner by phone or email.

Create an even better resume. (Or two. Or three ...) It's easy to get stuck on tactical questions when you create your resume and agonize about whether to include an objective statement, add college graduation dates, or mention hobbies. No matter what tactics you use, the applications of successful candidates share common characteristics.

Advice From an In The Know Portland Expert

Secret Sauce to a Kick-Butt Resume

by **Dawn Rasmussen** Chief Resume Designer and President of Pathfinder Writing and Career Services

Ask any Portland-area human resource manager, recruiter, hiring manager, or headhunter, and believe it or not, he or she will tell you that at least eighty-five percent of all resumes suck. I know ... I've asked them at the Portland Human Resource Management Association's conference and I've talked to HR volunteers helping out at the NW Youth Career Expo.

The good news is that there really is a simple solution to this common problem. It's all about shifting your perspective. You may think this document is all about you … but the truth is, it's *really* about them—them being the employer who is reading your document.

With this staggering statistic in mind, in order to get in the top ten percent of *awesome* resumes, your goal and mission is to start thinking about what you've done in the past and start positioning your accomplishments as value.

That means *not* simply including job duties underneath each employer.

You've got to do better than that.

Now is the time to start keeping track of on-the-job accomplishments. What have you done to make it better? What problems have you solved? How have you helped the company reach its goals? Make money, save money, save time?

Fear not, ye who have not kept track of such important things.

Many times, the answers to these questions lie in performance reviews, plans of work, staff reports, kudos letters, and any other recaps. If you don't have access to these documents, then your best guess is … your best guess. But always be honest. And be conservative.

The same thing goes for quantifying your results. You should always try to put a number on your accomplishment statements. That helps answer the other question that employers have when reading a candidate's resume: Based on what this person did for the previous employer, what is he or she going to do for me?

And that is the secret sauce to a kick-butt resume … when you can win them over with results, not fluff.

In addition to Dawn's excellent advice, here are more ideas and suggestions to keep in mind when you are creating or updating your resume.

- **Update your resume for every job.** Thanks to the Internet, a job opening today can attract hundreds of applications. To stand out, you need to revise your resume to match your accomplishments and skills for every job posting. Another reason to do this, as we mentioned above, is that many companies in Portland use tracking systems to scan resumes for keywords. Materials missing the relevant phrases never make it to human reviewers. So don't forget to include as many keywords as possible in the descriptions.

- **Keep it simple.** Good resumes adopt plain and simple design principles. Use classic fonts like Helvetica or Times New Roman for body copy, and apply bold and italic with restraint. Boxes, screens, and other flashy tricks can distract readers and confuse automated scanners. Keep it simple and easy to read.

- **Avoid age bias.** Laura Schlafly, founder of Career Choices with Laura and a frequent *Mac's List* blog contributor, specializes in working with midlife professionals. She suggests avoiding age discrimination by deleting the following items.

  - An objective statement: Skip it and instead state how you'll help solve problems.

  - "References Available Upon Request:" Omit this completely.

  - Complete chronological resume: Don't list every job you've had, with your title and duties. Instead, show relevant skills, work ethic, leadership, and problem-solving abilities.

  - Old email domains: Get rid of AOL, EarthLink, Teleport, and other once-popular email address domains introduced in the 1990s that reveal your age.

- **Get professional help if you need it.** Have you had multiple interviews and no job offers? How about over ten years of work experience you're trying to cram into a one-page resume? Maybe it's time to consult a professional. Hiring a career-service provider is a personal decision, and while it may not be necessary for everyone, it can help when you feel stuck.

Resume writers, career coaches, career management coaches, and life coaches all charge a fee for their services but can be a lifesaver for someone who needs support, guidance, or resume-writing assistance. So how do you find someone who is right for you? Talk to at least three different people to see who is the best fit for you, then follow up by checking them out online. Find out how much they charge, but don't make your decision based on price alone. Look for someone you connect with and then go with your gut. Think of it as an investment. Don't be discouraged by the fees that writers and coaches charge, because in the end you'll get what you pay for.

Follow the rules of the application process and form. All Oregon state jobs require the completion of a standard form. This may also be true of some city and county jobs. Each public agency's human resource office reviews your application and assigns a score. The ranking you receive depends on the words you use and how closely the text in your application matches a position description.

How to Get an Oregon Government Job: Four Lessons Learned

by **Mac Prichard**   Founder of Mac's List and President of Prichard Communications

Before starting my own public relations company, I had the good fortune to work as a communications officer in Oregon state and local government and at Portland State University. I had some wonderful jobs, including stints in the governor's office and Portland City Hall.

Here are four lessons I learned for you to consider when applying for a government job in Oregon.

Pay attention to key words. A human resource office assigns your application a score. The ranking you receive depends on the words you use and how closely your application text matches a position description. Long ago a veteran state employee advised me to highlight keywords in a job posting and make sure I used the same phrases. Once I did, my scores went up and I received more interviews.

Respect deadlines (or else). Here's an embarrassing story. Back in 1991 when I lived in Boston, I applied for a communications job with an Oregon school district. On the first day of a business trip, the phone rang in my hotel room. The caller, an assistant at the Oregon school district, had tracked me down and asked me to respond in writing to a set of questions by Friday. The Internet did not exist, I had no computer, and I had five days of meetings ahead of me.

I told the assistant I would fax her my essays after the Friday deadline. Big mistake. When I called weeks later, I learned that I was not a candidate. Deadlines are a big deal, especially in government.

Take a job no one wants. In the spring of 1994, I accepted a temporary stint managing public relations for the Oregon Driver and Motor Vehicle Services Division (DMV). I was probably the only person in Oregon who wanted the job. For months, the media had reported about a stalled overhaul of the DMV's computers. The project was $50 million over budget and had pushed wait times at DMV offices to more than three hours.

It was one of the best gigs I've ever had because the leadership team at DMV had a plan to reduce wait times. This made my job as a communicator easier because I was explaining how my employer was solving the problem.

Networking still matters. Most government jobs rely on a formal application process. Yes, you need to score high on written tests. It also helps to know interviewers through informational interviews and involvement in professional groups.

Networking counts most if you want a staff job with an elected official. I've worked for two: Earl Blumenauer (when he was a Portland city commissioner) and John Kitzhaber (in his first term as Oregon governor). I learned about both positions through informational interviews and networking meetings.

Want to learn more about public employment in Oregon? Visit the State of Oregon job page. Emerging Local Government Leaders' excellent website also has a careers section and good information about Oregon's public sector jobs. (See the end-of-chapter resource list.)

Create a professional portfolio.

If your work lends itself to a "show-and-tell" presentation, consider creating a professional portfolio. Even if at first glance it doesn't seem like your experience is all that visual, you may still be able to come up with ways to illustrate what you do. Adding images to your career accomplishments creates an additional layer of information and appeal for potential employers.

- **Tell your story.** Tell your career story in a way that is concise, on point, and engaging. A portfolio is a visual aid to help you tell your story—not a substitute. Pointing to examples of your work is great, but you must practice your pitch so that you don't ramble or rely too heavily on the portfolio to drive the conversation.

- **As in your cover letter and resume, point to the bottom line.** Potential employers always want to know how you can solve their problems. So it is important, even in a portfolio, to show that. Did you implement a social media strategy for a nonprofit? Quantify your success and highlight *in your portfolio piece and in your presentation* how your projects helped achieve company objectives. Did your social media strategy grow awareness or raise money? Showcase the outcome in a way that demonstrates your value as an intern or an employee.

- **Make an e-portfolio in addition to a physical one.** Don't simply create the traditional portfolio in print form; work up an online e-portfolio so that potential employers can just click on something. There are many sites where you can get help, such as Electronic Portfolios. (See the end-of-chapter resource list.)

Understand how recruiters work.

At some point during your career, you will probably get a call or an email from a recruiter or headhunter. Ironically, you may tend to hear from them frequently when you are not looking for work, yet find you can't catch their attention at all when you're in the middle of a job search.

What you need to know about recruiters is that they work directly for clients who are paying them to find qualified candidates. They are not in the business of serving as a career coach or counselor. Yet sometimes, when the moon is right and the planets are in the correct alignment, their needs may line up with your needs and you may suddenly find yourself in a mutually beneficial situation.

Arnie Fertig, head coach at JobHunterCoach, interviewed Brett Harwood of Portland's G4recruiters for the *Mac's List* blog. In the interview, Brett shared his suggestions for job seekers who want to attract the attention of headhunters in their field.

- **Be proactive.** Brett's number-one tip for job hunters: be proactive and don't rely on emails or online resume submissions alone. If you want recruiters to help you, help them by providing a list of the top twenty companies where you'd like to work and explain why.

- **Put yourself on YouTube.** He also advises that if you are hunting for a job, you should make a two-minute video of yourself. Post it on YouTube, and provide a link to it at the bottom of your resume. By doing so, you can communicate why you should be taken seriously and present your accomplishments, skills, and value. When recruiters and hiring managers view your video, they will have the ability to judge how you present yourself: your voice, enthusiasm, body language, and overall personality.

- **Pay for the premium account on LinkedIn.** Once you do, not only can you see the full list of who's looked at your profile, but recruiters outside your network will be able to contact you. And that's in addition to the other benefits offered by the premium membership. Yes, it's $29.95 per month, but for many people it is more than worth it.

- **Pick up the phone.** Brett makes upward of fifty calls a day to people he's dealt with over the years. He also receives ten to twenty unsolicited resumes a week but barely looks them over and rarely calls in response. But, he says, "If you take the initiative and pick up the phone and call me, I'll talk." The bottom line: regardless of today's technologies, nothing beats the tried-and-true method of picking up the phone and making human-to-human contact. The direct approach is also a great way to demonstrate your interest and hunger to succeed.

Dig deeper!

For links to some of the topics covered in this chapter (including cover letter and resume tips, state jobs in Oregon, electronic portfolios, local recruiters, *Legally Blonde* and scented resumes, and tall bikes in Portland, among many others), go to www.macslist.org/references.

6 Interviewing and Marketing Yourself

Courtesy matters!

It's true—and we've got the survey data to back it up. Portland has the most courteous drivers in the United States. It's an impressive feat, especially considering the amount of coffee most locals consume on a daily basis. (Another survey gives Portland the title of the third most-caffeinated city in the U.S., right after Anchorage and Seattle.) And your horn? Don't even think about using it unless you are honking in solidarity as you drive past some local protesters!

When it comes to job interviews, it's just like your mother told you—it never hurts to be polite. Focusing on the interviewer's time, needs, and perspective gives you an edge on your competitors while showing that you are both a courteous and strategic career professional. Want to nail your next job interview? Here's what to do before, during, and after that important meeting or phone call.

Prepare yourself for the interview.

Do your homework ahead of time in order to set yourself up for a successful interview.

Find out about the person you are meeting. It's acceptable to ask who will interview you. Study the biographies and blogs of your interviewers and visit their social media accounts. Look for shared interests and common connections. People want to work with people they know or who are known to people they trust, so keep an eye out for a mutual friend or colleague who can serve as a reference. Building this kind of rapport makes a manager more comfortable with you.

Understand what an employer needs. Employers hire people to solve problems, and candidates who understand this always stand out. Talk about how you can make an employer's life easier before you discuss how a job meets your personal and professional goals. Don't forget to consider the hiring process from the perspective of the employer. You'll be a much stronger candidate if you remember that a company has a set of problems that you may be ideally suited to solve.

Also remember that as you sit down for your job interview, one or more of the following unspoken topics are likely to be on an employer's mind:

- **Culture fit trumps expertise.** Being the smartest person in the room isn't enough to land the job. Employers put personality traits ahead of technical skills, so look for ways to show how you understand and fit into a company's culture.

- **"I needed someone two months ago!"** A hiring process can be like a home remodel project: it often takes twice as long as planned. As a result, employers may be in a hurry to make up for lost time.

- **The work is piling up.** Whether a job is a new or an old position, it exists because it meets a need. In other words, important tasks, some now perhaps urgent, aren't being completed and clients may be dissatisfied.

- **The staff is unhappy doing two jobs.** Only so much work can be postponed. In the meantime, current staff—perhaps already stretched thin—has to plug the gap, adding more pressure to hire sooner rather than later.

- **The field of candidates is small.** Yes, hundreds of people may have applied. Don't let those odds intimidate you, however. Those applicants aren't in the running anymore.

Research the company, agency, or organization. Find out whatever you can about the place where you are seeking employment. Search to identify the challenges it faces and prepare examples of how you have handled similar problems. Look for specific information about its products, policies, and practices so that you can ask specific and strategic questions during your interview.

Prepare and practice. Identify the key questions you think you will be asked, about both the job and your skills. Many websites have example interview questions. (See the end-of-chapter resource list for two of them.) Practice interviewing and answering questions in front of your friends or a mirror for at least twenty minutes. A mirror can help assure that you are making eye contact and not fidgeting. Or tape your rehearsal and watch the playback.

Interviewers tend to use three common themes to generate questions.

- **"Why you?"** Think about why you deserve the job over other applicants. Consider what skills you can offer and what problems you can solve.
- **"Why did you apply for this job?"** Don't simply say you need the money— think deeper about your short- and long-term career goals.
- **"Why are you interested in this company?"** Research the company and what it does. Employers want someone who is enthusiastic about the company and can bring something new.

Come with your own questions. Bring a list of questions, especially ones that focus on an employer's and organization's needs. You'll show that you are putting their concerns first while creating an opportunity to explain how you would tackle those challenges.

Dress to impress. Dress business casual or research the company to see whether a suit is necessary. Offices are much less formal these days, so business casual works most of the time. Always know the office culture, however. Avoid being too casual, and, above all, do not show up to an interview after you've just worked out. You might as well not show up at all!

Advice From an In The Know Portland Expert

How to Pick the Right Interview Outfit

by **Cecilia Bianco**   Former Community Manager at Mac's List

You've done your research and you understand the company culture as best as you can. Here's your first test: pick an interview outfit that proves it!

If the company culture seems laidback, as many Portland agencies are, wear something that shows you understand and appreciate this, but don't over- or under-do it! The other employees might be in jeans and cotton tees, but this is still an interview.

Dark, more formal jeans are acceptable as long as they are paired with the right top. For women, I suggest a silk button-down or a shirt with an appropriate neckline and a blazer on top. For men, a button-down polo (make sure it is ironed!) with or without a blazer on top will do the trick!

If the company culture seems formal, go all out to show you recognize—and will fit into—this atmosphere.

As a woman, you can't go wrong with a pantsuit or the timeless skirt and blazer combo. Dresses are acceptable, too, as long as you're paying attention to the neckline and the hemline. Keep it at the collarbone and just below the knee. Make sure the fabric gives you a polished and put-together look—no cotton and, for goodness' sake, no flannel, unless you're interviewing at ADX Portland, of course!

For men, get yourself into a business suit—whether you rent or buy one. If you end up getting the job, you can count on buying at least one suit to meet the dress code anyway, so why not find one that fits well and gives you confidence before the interview? If your budget or your comfort refuses to play by this rule, then I suggest black slacks, your nicest long-sleeve button-down, and a tie.

General rule for shoes: Regardless of a formal or informal office culture, avoid wearing overly casual open-toe shoes to any interview. Flip-flops will make a bad impression, but peep-toe heels are acceptable for women, especially in spring and summer. Make sure they are clean and presentable. While many Portland agencies will accept you wearing Vans or Converse, they had better not be scuffed up or have holes—and don't even bring Birkenstocks with socks into the conversation!

The outfit you wear to your interview should make you feel confident, polished, and comfortable. Don't choose something that doesn't feel like "you" or makes you feel like you're dressing up for an acting role. Portland employers tend to be more lenient with dress code, and the most important thing is to demonstrate that you care enough to **dress to impress**!

Arrive on time, but don't arrive too early. Don't get there more than five minutes before an appointment. You don't want to add additional pressure to your interviewer's already packed schedule.

Don't forget your resume. Offer to share your resume before you begin. It's a good way to break the ice and gives the interviewer the chance to refresh his or her memory without having to be obvious about it.

Breathe! Take a few deep breaths while you are waiting. Concentrate on your breathing rather than your nerves to set your mind at ease. If you have the chance, go to the bathroom or a private space and stand for two minutes with your arms overhead and your legs apart, making your body into a large X shape. This expansive pose can cause a spike in testosterone and a drop in cortisol, which can lead to feelings of calm empowerment. (For yoga lovers, another good option is the Goddess Pose, which is said to energize the body and encourage mental toughness.)

Remember that you got the interview for a reason. The hiring committee already saw something promising about you, so don't let your nerves keep you from landing your dream job!

Make the most of your interview.

Follow these tips to make a great first impression, whether on the phone or in person.

Know how to handle a phone interview. Employers often screen applicants with a phone interview. Not only are they making sure you're sane and reasonably intelligent, they also want to make sure both the candidate and employer are on the same page regarding location, salary, availability, and qualifications.

A phone interview can be an easy task to underthink, given the informality of a phone call and the casual location in which you may be taking the call. Here are three suggestions to help you perform well during phone interviews.

- **Walk, stand up, or sit up straight in a chair.** Choose whatever pose it takes to keep you active, dynamic, and focused. Lounging, laying, sprawling, or anything that feels relaxed and casual will come out that way in your voice.

- **Prevent interruptions.** This may sound like a *duh*, but it's important to take care of the small things. Will outside noises disrupt you? Is your dog going to bark at the mail carrier? Is somebody going to send you a mass of texts? Small things can distract both you and the interviewer.

- **Limit computer distractions.** Keep your computer at the ready during a phone interview, providing easy access to your resume, a job description, and background on the company or interviewer. But don't let anything else happen on your computer screen. Videos, music, email, and Twitter feeds distract you, so turn them off.

Use your interview to learn about the office culture. In an in-person interview, you are there for the interviewer to meet and evaluate you and your skills, but don't forget that you are also there to evaluate your interviewer and the workplace. Use your interview to learn about the office and to take a hard look around you.

Although viewers of *Portlandia* might think otherwise, the culture of Oregon's workplaces varies widely. Not every office—even in Portland—is filled with young creatives who bring their pets to work. Whether you're applying at a startup firm or a traditional top-down company, it's important to learn as much as you can about a workplace's culture both before and during a job interview. Understanding a manager's style, how staff relate to each other, and what the office environment is like help you present well and make an informed decision about a job offer.

In addition, how a company organizes and runs a job selection process can say a great deal about its daily operations. Here are three areas to observe during the interview process that can give you insights into how a workplace functions and whether it's a good fit for both you and your potential employer.

- **Punctuality: Is the interviewer on time?** If you are kept waiting for more than forty minutes for a job interview while the manager checks his or her phone, you might want to think twice. That kind of tardiness speaks volumes about how a person might work with employees.

- **Workplace:** Are you comfortable working in a bullpen, or do you prefer a workspace of your own? Be sure to see where you will work before accepting an offer.

- **Collaborative vs. competitive:** Some people thrive in a competitive atmosphere. Others prefer a collaborative environment. Be clear about your own preference and what the potential employer offers. Need more information about office culture and the interview process? The Office of Human Resources at Portland State University has a list of seven questions about office culture that job applicants should ask and interviewers should be prepared to answer. (See the end-of-chapter resource list.)

Stick to your talking points during the interview. Remember all that prepping and self-evaluation you did before the interview? Put it in play and show your interviewer that you've done your research, you've already analyzed how your skills and experience fit the position, and you're ready to learn more. Here are three ways to keep the interview on the right track.

- **Demonstrate knowledge.** Remember, this is not just an interview but also a conversation about you as a potential employee. Show your interest in the company by discussing transitions, challenges, and successes that the organization has experienced. Doing this in a dynamic and conversational way not only signals that you've done your homework but also reflects your confidence. Phrases like "Correct me if I'm wrong, but I see that . . ." or "I may be mistaken, but in my research it appears that . . ." open the dialogue for a conversation that positions you as eager to learn and to help.

- **Point to strengths.** Maybe you're a great networker, a genius at streamlining processes, or a wonderful project manager. Whatever your skills may be, now is the time to describe how those strengths apply to this job. Don't be shy. Employers want to hire people who have put thought into their career decisions. Show them that you are eager to put your strengths and skills to work on their behalf.

- **Solve problems.** Get creative if you have to, but it is important to show that you understand an employer's needs. Don't know a company's budget or its strategic plan? Look at historical data, ask questions, and think on your feet to come up with solutions to an organization's problems.

Don't get rattled by hard questions. It's not an urban legend—hard questions do happen in job interviews. Glassdoor, an online career community and database, recently released a list of the top twenty-five oddball questions that job candidates were asked. "On a scale from one to 10, rate me as an interviewer" and "What song best describes your work ethic?" are real examples of these curveballs.

Why do they ask such hard questions? According to Samantha Zupan at Glassdoor, "Employers are looking to understand how candidates think, how they process and approach difficult brainteaser questions, and how candidates think on their feet when in a stressful situation."

If you are asked some of these kinds of questions, keep your sense of humor as well as your sense of perspective. Here are a few questions from the list and some suggestions on how to answer them.

- **"How many cows are in Canada?"** Employers aren't looking for a correct answer. Really. Who knows how many cows are in Canada? So think your way through these hard questions with creativity. Show your problem-solving skills by saying, "I would need some time to research this, but I assume there are two cows for every vegan and one cow for every vegetarian in Canada." It's a pithy answer and demonstrates a sense of humor as well.

- **"What kitchen utensil would you be?"** Coming up with an answer to an absurd question like this shows how you can think on your feet and act with courage. Wow your interviewer by saying, "Based on my research, I believe that your company would be a spoon and the one thing every spoon needs is a fork. With soup always comes a salad, no? I'd be a fork."

However you answer, don't stress out! Take a deep breath. Pause for a moment. Show that you've researched the company, that you're the best candidate for the job, that you're cool under pressure. As Han Solo says, "I don't know. Fly casual."

When in doubt, pivot and redirect. Pivoting is a technique commonly used to dodge a question in a diplomatic way. Pivot when an interviewer asks you a question you don't feel entirely comfortable answering, for whatever the reason may be. Experts in pivoting do it subtly enough that the interviewer hardly notices the shift in conversation. Watch political debates and you'll see politicians doing this with great skill.

For example, let's say an interviewer asks you about a gap in your employment and you don't really want to reveal that during that year you were going through a divorce and wallowing in your sorrows at a retreat center on a deserted island. This is when pivoting can be useful. Respond by saying, "That was a time in my life when I was doing personal exploration and it ultimately led me to apply to the MBA program from which I just graduated."

Asking a question in return is also a skillful way to pivot. "Have you ever wished you could just take a year off and hide out on a deserted island? Well, I was taking advantage of a period in my life when I could do just that." Pivot to avoid responding to challenging questions when you don't want to divulge the entire back story or share experiences that you feel are too personal.

Use nonverbal factors to influence others. Did you know that your words account for only seven percent of how people judge you? It's true. Body language and presentation are the most significant ways people make assumptions about who you are. In a job interview, planning and preparation are important, but nothing compares to showing confidence as you head into that room. Your interviewer will decide how competent and likable you are in a fraction of a second, so your body language and facial expressions are crucial to your success. (See the end-of-chapter resource list for tips on projecting powerful nonverbal cues.)

Use body language to influence yourself. Amy Cuddy, a social psychologist and an associate professor at Harvard Business School, has spent years studying the power of our bodies to change our minds. She says that not only do you have to fake it till you make it, but she also encourages you to "fake it till you become it." Amy's research shows that the more space we take up with our bodies, the more powerful we feel and the more empowered we become.

According to Cuddy, if our nonverbal actions govern how we think and feel about ourselves, they undoubtedly affect how others see us. So it's important to be in control of our nonverbal cues in any social situation, but especially in an interview.

Stay curious. Most experts agree that employers love a candidate who is intellectually curious. When explaining how you solved a problem at a previous job, give examples of how you used your curiosity to fix it. This shows employers that not only are you an inquisitive individual, but that you know how to use it to your advantage and, most importantly, to their advantage.

Those questions you prepared before the interview? Now's the time to ask them. Almost every interview ends with the question, "Do you have any questions for me?" Show your preparation and interest in the position by asking away.

Learn how the job selection process works. When you ask your interviewer what happens next, it empowers you. It's also a question most employers expect interview candidates to ask. Ask for a detailed description of the decision-making process once the first round of interviews is complete.

Finally—and most importantly—ask for the job! *Do not end that interview without saying how much you want the job.* "Thank you for your time. I want you to know that I am very excited about this position and that I really want this job! When can I expect to hear from you?" In sales there's the old saying, "Always make the 'ask' and attempt to close the sale," and this is true in an interview, too.

Wait—you're not finished yet!

What you do after the interview is almost as important as what you did during it. Seal the deal with your post-interview followup.

Best Ways to Follow Up After the Interview

by **Jenny Foss**   Career Strategist, Voice of JobJenny.com,
Founder of Ladder Recruiting Group

You just finished the interview, and you nailed that sucker. But now, a couple of weeks have gone by and nothing's happened. Can you follow up without reeking of desperation or looking like a pest?

This topic freaks out a lot of job seekers. Many people, even when they know the interview went well, would rather do nothing than risk looking stupid or making the wrong move.

But staying top of mind is incredibly important—and not just for the job at hand. Even if you're not the right candidate now, wowing the decision maker can be incredibly valuable down the line.

So, how to finesse the "staying in touch" part of the process?

Ask about next steps (before you leave the interview). It stuns me that so few people end with this question. If you ask the interviewer what happens next, you know exactly when to follow up. If she says she'll be contacting candidates within a week, and it's day nine? It's completely OK to touch base and remind her of that timetable. Don't be pushy, but a quick note is perfect.

Get that thank-you note out (with lightning speed). I encourage job seekers to get out thank-you notes (to each individual they've met) immediately. Same day. From your laptop in the parking lot, if you really want to wow them.

Ask if you can connect via LinkedIn (and then do). It's perfectly appropriate to connect on LinkedIn after the interview, but you don't want to ambush anyone or leave the decision maker wondering what your motives are. Instead, create a reason for connecting, then ask if she's OK with it while you're at the interview.

An example: "You want to start dragon boat racing? I'd love to introduce you to my colleague. He leads a dragon boat team here in Portland."

Once you're linked, you can build a long-term relationship with that person, whether you land the job or not.

If things drag out, check in (periodically). The periodic check-in is the job-search technique people tend to stink at the most. But it's so important that it should be used throughout your career to keep your network fresh and engaged.

This is not about harassment: "Did I get the job?" "Did you make a decision?" It's about offering something of value to your contact. In doing so, you will also remind your interviewer that you're still out there. This could mean forwarding an article that you think she'll find interesting or congratulating her if she's earned some sort of recognition. Keep it simple and brief, and don't ask for anything back. If that person hears from you and has an update? She'll absolutely be in touch.

So, in summary… what Jenny said! And one more thought. Remember how in Chapter 5 we told you to check in with your references after you have an interview? Well, now's the time to do it. If you think it is likely that your interviewer will be in touch (and even if you don't think it's likely), it's a good idea to touch base with your references. Tell them about the job you interviewed for, the person you interviewed with, and which of your skills and experience you would like them to emphasize if the interviewer calls them. And don't forget to thank them—again!— for acting as your reference.

Negotiate like a pro.

Got a job offer? Congratulations! Now get ready to negotiate and don't forget …

You need to know local salary ranges for the position. Many factors influence the salaries in Portland, including education and local cost of living. There's one step we should all take when considering a salary offer—know what the local market pays. Here are four Oregon websites to help you learn what your coworkers and professional peers earn.

- **Glassdoor.com:** In addition to its list of oddball interview questions, this site also offers salary information for Oregon and other states. The data is posted anonymously by employees and job seekers, and you can search by city, state, job title, or company.

- **Oregon Employment Department**: Though best known for managing unemployment benefits, this state agency has a large team of economists and researchers who produce a steady stream of valuable reports and newsletter articles about Oregon's economy. Wages and salary information organized by location and profession is available online.

- **Oregon Nonprofit Sector Report:** This is required reading for anyone interested in working in Oregon nonprofits. Besides basic data about revenues, size, and organizational practices, this report also includes a table with average wages in nine nonprofit industries.

- **Oregon state employee salary information:** Applying for a state job? The Cascade Policy Institute has a searchable database of public records with salaries for state jobs and employees.

You don't have to accept the first proposal. Be reasonable, of course, but know that most employers expect you to negotiate on salary, benefits, and other issues. When possible, try to negotiate additional salary or benefits when the opportunity presents itself. Here are three techniques to use in your salary negotiations.

- **You need to separate the people from the problem.** Salary is a very personal matter, so emotions like fear, frustration, or anger can arise. Addressing the issues without damaging the relationship is the most important goal. So first try to understand the source of any emotions that come up. Work to address the root of the feeling (underappreciation, a misunderstanding, etc.).

  Before you go into a negotiation, carefully examine your company's or manager's point of view, including goals and obstacles. Knowing the other side's perspective is crucial to negotiation and can help you to distance yourself from issues that might at first seem personal.

  Communication in negotiation is important. Be an active listener and occasionally summarize the other person's points by saying, "So what I hear you say is ..." to sidestep misunderstandings. Avoid reacting, take your time, breathe, and don't be afraid to sit in silence while you think out your talking points before you speak.

- **Focus on interests, not positions.** In his book *Getting to Yes*, Roger Fisher explains that positioning yourself on a number or an outcome at the start puts the other party on the defensive, which can be a roadblock to successful negotiation. Avoid this trap by explaining your interests and giving the other person the opportunity to do the same.

An interest could be something like, "I want to feel that I'm valued here," or "Quality of life is really important to me." Pay attention to their interests, too, and work toward creative solutions that fulfill the interests and needs of both parties, or find places where there might be an opportunity for mutual benefit.

If an employer won't budge on salary, consider asking for the chance to work from home once a month, for a cell-phone reimbursement or a bus pass, or for whatever creative solutions you feel will help to meet your needs or promote your interests. These might be ways for you to compromise in some areas where your supervisor has wiggle room.

- **Ask for more time to think about it.** Finally, this might be the greatest tip of all. Negotiation can be exhausting and there might be some back and forth, so don't hesitate to ask for a day or two to think about it. Give a specific time when you'll have a decision, consider the offer, and if you want to continue negotiations, ask for another meeting to discuss.

If you walk into a negotiation and you feel blind as to what to expect from your boss or new employer, get his or her side and then ask for time to think about it. Say you need to speak with your spouse or partner, your mentor, or whomever (it doesn't matter), and go home and consider your options.

By all means, if they shove a piece of paper at you with a number on it, don't sign right away. Give yourself some time to noodle on it. If you feel you've been underbid right from the start and they won't budge on anything, ask for the opportunity to renegotiate your salary, benefits, or contract in six months. It can't hurt!

Dig deeper!

For links to some of the topics covered in this chapter (including sample interview questions, pivoting and body language during job interviews, salary information, the Goddess Pose, and The Driver's Seat Road Rage Survey, among many others), go to www.macslist.org/references.

7 Creating and Marketing Your Brand

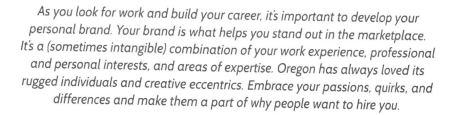

Work it, work it, work it!

Meet Brian Kidd, also known as the Unipiper. He's on a one-man campaign to keep Portland weird. As he says, "People are constantly telling me how I've become a symbol for this city, and as long as that holds true, I have a great responsibility." Whether he is impersonating Darth Vader, Gandalf, Jack Sparrow, Super Mario, or Santa Claus, the Unipiper knows his branding—a unicycle and bagpipes (along with a hefty dose of weirdness thrown in for good measure.

As you look for work and build your career, it's important to develop your personal brand. Your brand is what helps you stand out in the marketplace. It's a (sometimes intangible) combination of your work experience, professional and personal interests, and areas of expertise. Oregon has always loved its rugged individuals and creative eccentrics. Embrace your passions, quirks, and differences and make them a part of why people want to hire you.

Find the culture fit.

We Portlanders are not only rightly proud of our city's beautiful bridges and our famous food carts, but also of our people. Portland attracts dreamers, artists, and other individuals who are looking for a fresh start in a unique culture.

Whoever you are, you are likely to find your niche in Portland. Yes, amazing people flock here and compete for jobs in a difficult economy, but in the long run we all win when we live in a community where people seek work inspired by their passions. Knowing your strengths, your motivations, and your values will serve you well in this town. Portlanders love a good authentic story. Be yourself, not someone else. Stay true to your story and you will be rewarded.

Get Ahead in Portland by Being Unprofessional

by **Brittany Bennett** Project Manager at Substance,
Co-founder of WebBrand Agency

In 2010 I returned to Portland after spending five years working in Scottsdale, Arizona, and experienced a culture shock. The business community in Scottsdale is dramatically more conservative than it is in Portland, meaning that I used to wear nylons and blazers to work even when it was over 100 degrees outside.

I am self-employed, so I spend a lot of time shaking hands, kissing babies, and, most importantly, attending networking events. The first time I attended a networking event in Portland I wore my best black suit and a strand of pearls.

New to the PDX creative scene, I was desperate for others to see me as an established professional and take me seriously. I was stiff and rigid. I was all business.

After the event, a good friend of mine pulled me aside and told me that my work wardrobe needed a makeover. Horrified, I defended my ensemble, "But this is from *Nordstrom!*" My friend laughed and replied, "It doesn't matter how much you paid for it. You looked like an insurance agent and no one wanted to talk to you."

At the time, I was too busy being offended and judging his graphic tee to really hear him, but after I properly licked my wound, I realized the man had a point. And his point extended beyond my wardrobe.

Authenticity matters more than professionalism. Being professional is important, but being overtly professional can really work against you. Turns out, I was so uptight that I was not forming personal connections with any of my clients or contacts.

The truth is, it doesn't matter how good your portfolio is, how competitive your prices are, or how fast your turnaround time is; if someone doesn't like you, he or she is not going to choose to do business with you. Period. That's when I realized I needed to worry less about being professional and more about being authentic. Once I traded my suits for jeans and my collared shirts for graphic blouses, I felt more comfortable at work.

To succeed, you need to get personal. I also slowed down and realized that getting to know my colleagues and clients was an important part of the business process that should not be rushed. I asked about their families and hobbies. I took a genuine interest in *their* interests. Once I made this transformation, my business literally doubled.

Allow what you do professionally to be an extension of who you are personally. You will find that not only will you enjoy what you do more, but others will enjoy working with you more as well.

Create your personal brand.

As we've mentioned before, Portland is a metropolitan city that can feel like a small town. Spend enough time here and you'll find that while everyone may not know your name, they probably know someone else who does. And guess what? You have a personal brand whether you like it or not—and even if you're not sure exactly what it is.

Creating and developing your brand is useful at any stage of your career. It can be helpful when you are just starting out, as part of an overall self-evaluation (as described in Chapter 1), or as a means of making your first job a successful one. As you gain more job experience, personal branding plays an important role in helping you stand out in a crowded marketplace.

Start off on the right foot. When you finally land that job—either your first, a new one in a different field, or as a return after a long hiatus—you want to begin by creating a reputation as a top-notch professional. While Portland is definitely a less hierarchical place than New York City, for example, it's important to fit in and make the most of every opportunity. A successful brand starts with solid skills, great work experience, and fabulous word of mouth.

- **Be a savvy newbie.** Offer an outsider's perspective and raise new questions, but don't come on too strong or project too much of a "know-it-all" vibe for a beginner.

- **Be a bit of a social butterfly.** Set up get-acquainted meetings, coffees, or lunches with new coworkers and clients. They will teach you a lot and appreciate your curiosity.

- **Be a listener.** Yes, you have a lot to offer. But so do your new colleagues and customers. Listen to what they say about their problems and their ideas for fixing them.
- **Be the office historian.** Look ahead, not back, but understand where your organization has been. Talk to supervisors and colleagues about previous challenges faced by your new company and your predecessors. If you can, tap the wisdom and experience of others who have already done your job or similar ones.
- **Be an expert in the field.** Working in a central office or support function like communications or human resources? Get out into the field and talk to the people who provide the product you produce and to the people you serve. Learn everything you can about your new line of work.
- **Be an early achiever.** Try to identify an urgent need to solve in the first six months. Getting a big accomplishment under your belt quickly gives you credibility and authority.

Analyze your strengths and values. As you gain work experience and hone your skills, you are learning more about your abilities and interests. What do you like doing? What are you good at? What don't you like to do? What would you like to learn more about? Adding new abilities and areas of interest to your core skill set helps to expand your brand outside the confines of your job description and takes you in the direction you want to go.

Advice From an In The Know Portland Expert

Portland's Threads—and Yours

by **Aubrie De Clerck** Career coach and astrologer, Coaching for Clarity

In any search, it is up to us to tell our story—who we are, what we can do, and how we stand out doing it. Our story is not simply about identifying transferable skills. To find fulfilling work, we need to communicate our threads—the things we are best at, the things we can't stop doing even if we try, the things we do naturally, *our gifts*—in a way that creates confidence in ourselves and shows our value to an employer.

Take Portland as an example. We all know about keeping the city weird, but what is consistent about the town that filters into all the community does? What are

Portland's threads? Here are two: unrestrainable, creative self-expression and on-going commitment to environmental protection.

So how do we know with confidence that this is truly what Portland is about? If we were writing a resume for Portland, we would give specific examples.

- **Unrestrainable, creative self-expression**

  Food and drink: microbreweries, coffee roasters, adventurous award-winning restaurants, farmers markets

  Arts: International Film Festival, Jazz Festival, TangoFest, monthly art walks

  Annual events: Bridge Pedal, PDX Adult Soap Box Derby, Tour de Coops, Time-Based Art Festival

  Local businesses: Powell's Books, food carts, Hollywood Theater, Voodoo Doughnut

- **Ongoing commitment to environmental protection**

  Compost at the curb

  Sixty-three percent of all waste recycled

  Investment in public transportation

  Strong urban growth boundary

  Buffered bike lanes

  Leader in LEED-certified buildings

With clear examples identified, how do you assign value to them? What do these threads mean about Portland? To me, they create a great quality of life and keep our community vibrant—essential components for a city I choose to live in.

As you create your personal brand, ask yourself: "What are my threads? How do they give value to others?"

Promote your personal brand.

Once you've identified your personal threads and decided what they can contribute in your chosen field, you need to articulate that brand through unified messaging.

Social media: What you do and say on social media can strengthen or weaken your personal brand. Are you a job seeker with a bare-bones LinkedIn profile? You are sending a message to employers that you aren't serious about your profession. What are you saying on Twitter that employers or colleagues might learn about you? Social media is a huge contributor to your personal brand.

Positioning statement: This is how we want our audience to perceive, think, and feel about us versus the competition. Want to work in public relations for an art museum? Great! The more you understand your audience, the better you will be at positioning yourself for that new job. Think of it this way: *To (target audience)—I'm the applicant who offers (benefit) over others in this field. The reason is that (explain how your experiences or features relate to the benefit you can provide).*

Vision statement: This statement allows you to see where you are now and where you intend to be. This is what's called an internal communications piece—only for you to keep in the back of your mind. According to *The Science and Art of Branding* by Giep Franzen and Sandra Moriarty, "A vision statement is what a brand wants to be in the future and it consists of the brand's purpose and values." A solid vision for the future should guide you in setting your professional and life goals.

Elevator pitch: This is a very practical piece to nail down when looking for a job or networking. Create a concise and efficient elevator pitch that is an effective and memorable way to articulate your personal brand to new acquaintances. Walk the fine line between humility and confidence, but communicate your personal brand in an engaging way that gives a lasting first impression.

Professional bio: Whether it appears on your LinkedIn page, resume, or cover letter, a professional summary is your opportunity to use the keywords that define your personal brand. It typically draws upon your positioning and visioning statements to come up with a succinct narrative that distinguishes your personal brand from the competition.

Local expert Mike Russell of Pivotal Writing (see pages 97-98) writes about and offers workshops on professional bios, among other topics. Here are his top three suggestions for crafting a bio that will connect with future employers and clients.

- **Know your target audience.** Are you looking for nonprofit work? Maybe your passion is the environment? Or do you want to make a ton of money selling software? You *must* identify and speak to the audience you want to attract. As Mike says, "Speak as if you were addressing your ideal customer."

- **Talk to your target audience—this is not about you.** You must show how you can help your audience. "Shift the tone of your bio 10 degrees," says Mike, "and you can really change the effectiveness of your message." This is the difference between features and benefits—show how your "features" will "benefit" the target audience.

- **Leave a lasting impression.** "What is the *one story* that you want readers to remember after reading your bio?" asks Mike. Connect with the reader in an authentic way and you will distinguish yourself from your competition.

Advice From an In The Know Portland Expert

How to Ignite Your Professional Bio with a Killer First Sentence

by **M!ke Russell**   Mike Russell helps marketing managers of enterprise software businesses to generate qualified leads and accelerate sales with engaging, helpful content.

Portland loves quirky, colorful personality. Whether it's a bio statement on your website or your summary on LinkedIn, it had better start strong. Here's how to hook your reader's attention with that first sentence.

Be brazenly honest. What do you do better than anyone else? How have you stood apart from your coworkers or competitors in the past?

Clarify your target reader. Envision your favorite client or employer, and write to him or her. Since Portland loves to network, you may even be able to find a particular "target's" photo on LinkedIn. Think of him or her while you write.

Lead with your primary benefit. With so much going on in our beautiful city, it's easy for readers' attention to wander. Lead by answering their fundamental question: "What's in it for me?" Once you've hooked interest, you can you elaborate on whom you serve best, how, and why.

Examples

- **Rebecca the Small Business Lawyer**: "Rebecca Watkins of Willumbia Counsel ensures her small business clients receive the best outcome for their legal needs and the best advice for their money."
- **Paul the Chiropractor**: "Paul Allen of Catalyst Chiropractic fosters focus, pain relief, and stress reduction for people plagued by chronic discomfort."
- **Sarah the Life Coach**: "If Olympians, presidents, and CEOs rely on advisors, mentors, and teachers to succeed, don't you deserve a coach to help you unlock your full potential? Sarah Strauss, certified Life Coach with Achievement Today, will help you overcome self-limiting beliefs."

Say it loud and proud. This city prides itself on individualism and creativity. Assert your place in the community with confidence, even if it feels edgy. Portland wants to hear from you.

Website: Your website is an important part of your brand. It's a great place to advertise yourself and to refer potential clients and employers when they want to learn more about you. With a little time and effort, you can boost your professional presence online dramatically.

Here are four ways you can use a personal website to promote your brand.

- **Show and tell.** Your own website allows you to present information in greater depth than you can on your resume. With an online platform you can show past projects and writing samples and give a future employer the chance to see the details of what you have done.
- **Stay up to date.** Save time by refreshing your site and sharing your work right away. Provide an updated link to different prospective employers, or notify your LinkedIn followers that you have added something new to your webpage.
- **Share your personality.** A personal website allows for artistic freedom, and you can tailor it to your personal traits and preferences. Create a unique layout or logo, or provide an in-depth bio about yourself. This shows employers and future clients your taste and gives a sense of who you are.

- **Learn a new trade.** Launching and maintaining a website teaches you marketable technical skills. Popular publishing platforms like WordPress are are easy to use, but you still need know how to work with Cascading Style Sheets (CSS) and other online tools. Learning these techniques shows employers that you can teach yourself and catch on quickly. (Or, check out the free website-building sites in the end-of-chapter resource list.)

Visuals: You need to brand everything related to you and your career, whether it is your resume, your cover letter, your portfolio, your business card, your bio, or your website, with a consistent visual presentation. The unifed look helps to reinforce your brand wherever it is referenced. Here are three areas where your materials need to be consistent, clean, and appealing.

- **Color:** Pick a strong—but not overwhelming—color to use throughout the key materials that represent your personal brand. William Arruda, founder of REACH Personal Branding, suggests this scale to help choose the right color:

  Use **red** to express action, passion, power, or courage.

  Use **orange** to express determination, encouragement, strength, or productivity.

  Use **yellow** to express optimism, positivity, energy, or vision.

  Use **green** to express the environment, calmness, growth, or rebirth.

  Use **blue** to express trust, reliability, integrity, or truth.

  Use **purple** to express luxury, spirituality, inspiration, or dignity.

  To use color effectively in your materials, pick a signature area to do so and keep it simple. Common ways to incorporate color on your resume include underlining your name or having all of your job titles in your chosen color.

- **Font:** Choosing a signature font for your materials can be very beneficial to your brand. Make sure it is an easy-to-read font, even if you choose a serif font that shows a bit more personality in its curves or hooks than a simpler sans serif font. Avoid gimmicky fonts (hello, Comic Sans) or ones that may become dated too quickly. One way to combine a clean, readable font with a more unique font is to pick different areas for each. Your name or job titles are good areas for a quirky font; however, job descriptions and your contact info are two areas to keep plain and simple!

- **Format:** The format of your resume, cover letter, business card, e-portfolio, and even website (to whatever extent possible) needs to be consistent for your personal brand to ring clear. Font, color, and placement need to be the same throughout all materials. For example, if your resume has a vertical header with your name and contact information, then your other materials should have the same.

Turn your brand into self-employment.

As you develop your personal brand, you may find yourself succeeding so well at self-promotion that you begin to consider self-employment. Or you may have just become tired of working for someone else or of looking for the perfect job that never quite materializes. For many Oregonians, self-employment is a great alternative to working inside a company or other organization.

This option is especially attractive to Portlanders who love living here because of the high quality of life. Self-employment allows for a more flexible lifestyle and a routine that can exist outside the rigid nine-to-five workday. Whether it is part-time freelancing, a series of temporary full-time projects, or a full-time brick-and-mortar business, self-employment allows for more diversity in how you budget your time and money.

As with a job hunt, deciding to become self-employed requires some in-depth self-assessment and soul searching. There are many resources to guide you if you choose this path, but here are a few do's and don'ts to consider up front.

Do ...

- **Analyze the market.** You really, really, *really* need to understand the market—whether it is local, national, or international—for your goods or services. The only way to position and promote the value and benefits you bring to that market is to know it inside and out first.
- **Make friends with your competitors.** It may seem counterintuitive, but (as we keep mentioning) Portland is a small town. Even though you're competing in a general way, you've all got your own individual niches. So play nice. It's good karma. And it's also good business. Remember, your colleagues and competitors will be the first to refer to you when they can't handle their own overflow business or projects.

- **Brand yourself early on.** Branding is especially important in self-employment. Become the "go-to" person in your specialized field and then make that a prominent part of your brand. This is your way of standing out in that market you've just gotten to know so well.

- **Create a solid business plan.** Sometimes people ease their way into self-employment by starting with a side business—freelancing projects, selling something at a local market, or teaching a class. That's great, but once you decide to invest a lot of time and money into your business, you need a detailed financial plan. Work with a professional planner or have it reviewed by one. Your bottom line will thank you.

- **Budget carefully.** As you eagerly calculate your future earnings and dream of rolling around on a giant pile of cash, don't forget about the benefits that your former employer may have been paying on your behalf ... benefits such as health insurance, a retirement program, and—oh yes—the other half of your FICA contribution that you will now have to pay in full. If possible, create a cash reserve to tide you through several months. You need operating funds, and cash flow can become a major issue, especially if clients or customers don't pay you on time.

- **Know yourself and your work habits.** It's time to get real about what you can reasonably expect of yourself. Are you a night person? Then please don't set up a work schedule that regularly requires you to work early mornings. Likewise, don't plan to work alone at home if you know you need outside stimulation or if you're afraid you'll spend the entire day napping. Do you like to work by yourself? Do you need coworkers or colleagues? Create a work environment that plays to your strengths, while locking your weaknesses outside in the cold, cold rain.

- **Create a schedule.** Sure, you left your nine-to-five job to avoid the daily routine, but you still need a schedule. Sometimes it's the only thing that keeps you from spending the entire afternoon watching cute animal videos on YouTube. Try to plan your days and weeks so that you allow time for the work tasks themselves, in addition to other activities such as networking, self-promotion, client contact, communications ... and a life outside work.

- **Prepare to work more than you expect.** See previous point. Then double the amount of time you think you're going to need. Self-employment brings with it a huge amount of unpaid hidden or "shadow" work, such as managing employees, interacting with customers, attracting new business, keeping track of hours and inventory, invoicing, banking, paying taxes, and doing a wide variety of other administrative tasks.

Don't ...

- **Start a business if you're afraid of taking risks.** Remember that part about knowing yourself? There's no shame in being risk averse. But if you're planning to be self-employed, at least part of your nature needs to be willing to take the leap and embrace your inner daredevil, if only in a controlled and cautious fashion. If not, you may want to choose a more secure career path. (However ... do know that many experts believe that in the long run, self-employment offers the least overall career risk—you never have to fear being fired, laid off, or tortured by an incompetent boss who makes you so crazy you quit in despair.)

- **Try to do too much too fast.** Self-employment is exciting. You're doing what you want to do and doing it on your own terms. But just like a sneaker wave on the Oregon coast, things can change quickly. It's easy to get in over your head and not be able to handle the work in a timely fashion. Remember, you want your personal brand to stand for quality, reliability, and integrity, not "Uh, I meant to get that to you last week—how does first thing Monday morning sound?" Be fastidious about meeting deadlines and delivery dates.

- **Put all your eggs in one basket.** (Or at least don't do it without being aware of the potential downside.) Whenever possible, diversify. Try to get a broad base of clients. That way, if a client suddenly loses its budget or a sector of the economy takes a turn for the worse, you won't lose all your income in one fell swoop. That said, if you are making tons of money from a single source, congratulations! Don't fret about it too much, but do keep your eyes open to expanding your customer base whenever possible.

- **Isolate.** Even if you are a one-person show, you still need ideas, advice, and social contact. Make time to reach out to colleagues and other self-employed professionals, whether it is during an informal get-together or at a professional networking event.

- **Forget about up-front tax planning and retirement savings.** Depending on the kind of business you have, you will either pay quarterly estimated taxes or make a weekly or monthly payroll, which includes payroll taxes. For many first-time business owners, the cash flow associated with tax payments is a challenging issue.

  Depending on where you live in Oregon, there may be additional taxes for the self-employed (such as a City of Portland business license and Multnomah County and TriMet taxes), so you need to plan for those as well. And, as mentioned previously, the self-employed also pay both the employee and employer share of the federal FICA tax that funds Social Security and Medicare, instead of just the employee portion. A good bookkeeper or accountant can help you get a handle on your tax situation before it's time to file your tax forms. Remember, no one likes an ugly surprise come April!

  Finally, if you're self-employed, you need to think about your own retirement savings, such as a Simplified Employee Pension (SEP) or a 401(k) plan. The type of plan depends on what kind of business you set up. An accountant or retirement investment specialist can let you know which option is best for you.

And one more thing ... never stop learning. There are a lot of resources out there for people looking to set up their own businesses. Make sure you do as much research as you can before you make that leap! Take time to check out these Oregon-based resources.

- **Chris Guillebeau and *The $100 Startup*.** Portlander Chris Guillebeau writes about unconventional work, entrepreneurship, and foreign travel on his blog, *The Art of Nonconformity*. He has never held a regular job. Instead, he has found ways to turn his ideas into income that allows him to help others and travel frequently. His book, *The $100 Startup: Reinvent the Way You Make a Living, Do What You Love, and Create a New Future*, offers case studies, practical tips, and well-organized materials useful to everyone who wants find a way to get paid doing what they love. He also organizes the extremely popular World Domination Summit every July in Portland, which last year attracted creative people from twenty countries.

- **Location 180**: Portland resident Sean Ogle writes about how to build a business you can run from anywhere.
- **PortlandCreativeList**: This site seeks to connect Portland's creative professionals for the greater collective good. While perhaps best known for its very good job board, it also has a terrific resources page for the self-employed.

In addition, funding exists to help small businesses start up and prosper. Investigate the resources at Mercy Corps Northwest, Portland Incubator Experiment, and Kickstarter via the resource list on the Mac's List website. (See end-of-chapter resource list.)

Dig deeper!

For links to some of the topics covered in this chapter (including first job tips, personal branding, free website-building tools, taking a leap of faith, and the Unipiper, among many others), go to www.macslist.org/references.

8 Navigating Your Career Path

It's always under construction!

Portland is a magnet for DIYers. It seems like everyone you meet is working on a project, whether it is a soap box racer for the PDX Adult Soap Box Derby, a vegetable garden with a composting center and worm bins, or a full-on home remodel. And, as every true Portlander knows, almost every project will eventually lead to one place—Mr. Plywood. In the heart of the eastside Montavilla neighborhood, Mr. Plywood's distinctive sign has long served as a beacon to enthusiastic hobbyists and professional construction workers throughout the city and beyond.

Think of your career like a long, never-ending construction project—sort of like the roads and bridges in the greater Portland-metro area during the summer. (Kidding, just kidding!) But in your case, you can actually control its direction, movement, and timing. Even when work gets stressful and you can feel the demands piling up, it's good to poke your head up occasionally and take a look around. Remind yourself that your career is constantly moving and evolving. You can take it along the road you choose and, with any luck, avoid most of the potholes along the way.

Make conscious decisions about your goals.

Once you find a job and then maybe another one or two, it's easy to settle into a routine. And that's fine—as we all know, job hunting is stressful and you deserve a chance to relax and bask in the joy of your fabulous new career. Suddenly you have interesting professional responsibilities, fascinating coworkers, and ... an income! Hooray! Life is good.

But after some time has passed and the novelty wears off, you may find yourself wondering, "Is this it?" Maybe there are other areas you want to explore. Maybe your new job is a bit more stressful or time-consuming than you had hoped. Maybe it's not a good fit for your personal strengths and weaknesses. Or maybe you've just outgrown it.

Never stop assessing yourself and your values. The key to happiness in any career is to find an organization that shares your values and a job that allows you to use your strengths. In your career path, it is easy to forget that you, as the employee, are evaluating the company as much they are evaluating you. It's like dating—will this relationship be a good fit long term?

Is quality of life more important to you than a large paycheck? Do you hate team-work? Do you love networking or dislike sitting in an office? Do you want to do different things every day? Take the time to return to and answer the tough questions you learned to ask yourself back in Chapter 1.

If you are looking for a career that does more than pay the rent or mortgage, you need a more holistic approach to your career strategy. Kare Anderson, an Emmy award winner, former *Wall Street Journal* reporter, and University of Oregon graduate, addressed this issue in a talk at the University of Oregon School of Journalism and Communications George S. Turnbull Center in Portland. The gist of her advice was to build a set of values from which you operate and use them to guide you on your career path to opportunities that far exceed what's listed on a job board. Here are Kare's values for crafting a career.

- **"The sooner we get clearer about our top talent, the quicker we can hone in on it and offer value."** Figure out what your strength is—what you have to offer the world—and refine it. Hone in on it. Applying to jobs willy-nilly isn't a great idea. Be strategic about where you can use your talents and for what cause.

- **"Find allies. It's a hybrid world, so befriend people who have different talents than you."** Once you know your top talent, connect with others to understand where they shine. Ask questions. Be curious. You never know what you'll find out. Connect them with others. Share information. Help them and look for ways that they can help you. We'll all be better for it and it could lead to opportunities you've never considered.

- "Find the sweet spot of mutual benefit sooner rather than later." Look for the intersection of your talent with the talents of others, find where mutual benefit can be found, and innovate together for a more resourceful approach to your mission.

- Ask: "Whom do you draw closer to you? Whom do you admire the most and how do you honor them? Are you a giver, a taker, or a matcher?" Use these questions as a way to guide strategy for your career and your life goals.

What makes work meaningful? If having meaningful work is one of your values, remember that meaningful work can mean different things to different people. In order to understand what it looks like for you, ask yourself these questions:

- **What If working to put food on the table for you and your family may, in fact, make work meaningful?** You can find meaning in the results you produce, the coworkers you interact with, the mission you support, or the sheer fact that the money you make allows you to take care of your loved ones and yourself. Even the ability to pay off a large debt can give a job more meaning.

- **What if meaningful work is only an abstract concept that may elicit any combination of feelings such as satisfaction, comfort, gratitude, relief, stability, power, or influence at any given time?** Maybe your job isn't helping to save the rain forests or feed the homeless, but maybe it's helping you feel more secure? In your security, you might find that you're happier, kinder, and more thoughtful to your loved ones, which gives your life more meaning.

- **Is meaningful work found in the opportunity to use your best strengths and talents?** Tom Rath, author of *StrengthsFinder 2.0*, argues that when you do work that allows you to use your strengths, you're happier, more productive, and feel more satisfaction at the end of the day.

- **Maybe meaningful work is a combination of all of these ideas and concepts and it's up to us to figure out whether we're content in our present situation or if we long for more?** If so, what does more look like? Sometimes, as the poet Rainer Maria Rilke wrote, you have to "live the questions" to find the answers you seek. The longing for meaningful work is indeed a personal quest, unique to you and your own set of circumstances.

Four Principles to Guide Your Career

by **Ben Forstag** Managing Director of Mac's List

Careers develop continuously over the forty or fifty years of our working lives. They are subject to forces both internal (family dynamics, changes of interest) and external (the economy, the job market). Accordingly, I've always been dubious about "mapping out" an entire career in advance. The linear progressions of model career development—law school, clerkship, federal prosecutor, 9th Circuit, Supreme Court!—rarely play out so cleanly in real life.

I've certainly worked to navigate my career's direction. However, rather than targeting a predetermined destination, I've focused on the journey itself. My career plan is less a roadmap than it is a set of four practical guiding principles.

1. Do what you're good at. We've all heard the dictum "do what you love." This is great advice if you have strong passions and a clear vision of how to monetize them. But sometimes the things we love most don't translate into a job that pays the bills—at least not right away. In these situations, I urge people to focus first on their skills, rather than their passions—do what you do well!

Skills can transfer to different jobs, industries, and interests. Focusing on professional strengths gives you career flexibility, while also illuminating potential avenues for work in the field of your choice. And ultimately, passion and skill are two sides of the same coin. There's a reason you are good at some things and not others; your skill set is a reflection of the interest and enjoyment you derive from doing those activities. In this sense, doing what you're good at is actually a way to do what you love.

2. Keep learning. Taken by itself, the "do what you're good at" rule could lead to a static, monotonous career. That's why it's important to stay curious and explore new interests and skills. Read books and blogs, take classes, network outside your field—do anything that exposes you to new ideas. You may discover professional interests that you never imagined.

Throughout my own career, I have tried to say "yes" to learning opportunities whenever they appear. As a result, I've gained new passions for statistics, data analytics, and coding—a surprising development for someone who went out of his way to avoid math classes in college!

3. Stay balanced. It's good to be passionate about your job, but it's also important to have passions outside of the office. One of the best things you can do for your career is to have a healthy work/life balance which provides an escape valve for the stresses of work. It can also insulate you from the inevitable down periods in your professional life.

4. Live your own dream. This is the final rule, but perhaps the most important. You have to evaluate your career according to your own criteria—not anyone else's. Measuring yourself against other people's successes is like trying to live their dream, rather than your own. Try to focus on what you want and like to do without worrying about what others may think. Professional contentment is neither objective nor relative; the only question is whether your job and career path bring you happiness.

Create your career path. Then follow it. (Or vice versa.)

Analyze before acting. Sometimes you create your career path up front and follow it according to plan. Other times you look back at your footsteps and see that they have created a path of their own. Either way, at some point you need to stop and reflect on where you've been and where you're going.

Dawn Rasmussen (who offered some great resume tips in Chapter 5) has written a guide to career management, *Forget Job Security: Build Your Marketability!: Finding Job Success in the New Era of Career Management*. Her focus is on career management and how to foolproof your career in a volatile and fickle job market. Here are six steps she recommends you take to manage your career.

- **Define your purpose.** You need to know what you want. Being clear about your career goals helps you explain what you offer and ultimately helps you answer the question every employer asks, "What can you do for me?"

- **Know your value.** Successful career managers can explain the unique value they offer with a short statement that connects with an employer's wants, needs, and values.

- **Develop your brand.** If you don't develop a personal brand, employers and colleagues will do it for you. You need to identify your passions, strengths, and skills and turn these lists into a branding statement you can use in interviews and presentations.

- **Master the building blocks.** Everybody has to have a few basic career building blocks in place. These include adding new skills, paying attention to your reputation (especially online), and building value inside and outside an organization.

- **Keep your tools current.** Good career managers regularly update their resumes, work samples, and other application materials. They see these documents as dynamic and so are ready when an unexpected opportunity presents itself.

- **Shape your destiny.** Think and plan ahead. Be prepared for new opportunities (or layoffs) by taking classes, participating in industry organizations, mentoring others, and working to a career plan.

Advice From an In The Know Portland Expert

Lessons Learned by the Recently Unemployed

by **Marsha Warner**, SPHR Founder of Portland-based Career Factors, Career Coach, and Executive Recruiter

Recently, a client shared what he wished he'd done before he found himself on the job hunt. Here's a list of best practices for career maintenance that are applicable to everyone.

I wish I'd kept a copy of my performance reviews. *Lesson:* Keep your own file of reviews and accolades. They are helpful to prompt accomplishment statements, review for interviews, and to remind yourself of achievements when doubts creep in.

I wish I had continued to network and develop outside contacts. *Lesson:* Don't wait until you are unemployed to start networking. Stay in touch with colleagues, classmates, ex-bosses, other parents, fellow volunteers, and so on.

I wish I had joined LinkedIn earlier on. *Lesson:* Keep your LinkedIn profile active. It's a tool for recruiters, a way to stay connected, and a source of information for professional development. Spend an hour a week updating your profile, reconnecting, joining interest groups, and staying current.

I wish I had not taken it so personally; I let this layoff really get to me. *Lesson:* When your job ends, take time to mourn the loss and acknowledge your emotions, then let it go. Evaluate the job market, then take up your career toolbox and go forth. Know that when you are part of a reduction in force, it's a business decision, not a personal one. Take charge of your career with a personal marketing plan. Manage what you can control and let go of what you cannot.

I wish I had reached out and passed along my professional knowledge to younger colleagues before I left. *Lesson:* Teaching is a great source of career satisfaction. Some companies have formal programs for knowledge transfer. Seek them out. The effort will be worth the reward you'll feel in sharing your knowledge with others.

I wish I had paid more attention to my own development and taken advantage of challenges that would give me more exposure. *Lesson:* Proactive career management means stepping up to challenges. Volunteering for projects and committees or getting training for new skills are ways to grow. They get you noticed by your boss and bring greater satisfaction to your daily work. Ask yourself at the end of each day, "What did I learn today?"

I wish I had asked for help early on in my job search. Things have changed so much; I feel a bit lost. *Lesson:* Feeling isolated and lost is common. A career coach can offer expert information and advice about the job market and how to put your best foot forward. Portland is blessed with great career resources, including local colleges, private coaches, and job-search support groups. Help is available. Be wise and ask for it.

Know when it's time to start looking again. The key question to ask yourself is, "Do you feel stuck?" If so, it's time to think about making some changes. While the best decisions we can make for ourselves are also often the hardest, sometimes the most difficult decision you can make is the best decision for you.

Here are five signs that you're stuck and what you can do about it.

- **You feel paralyzed.** Do you pursue jobs, projects, or professional relationships only to be caught between a yes and a no? Do you feel like you're standing in the middle of a foreign town without a map? The inability to make a decision can feel paralyzing. If this is how you feel, stop spinning your wheels, bring your attention to the current events in your life, and ask yourself this: What is holding you back? Go with your gut answer and don't be afraid to acknowledge it (if only to yourself at first).

- **You feel uninspired.** Do you just sit in a chair at the end of the day and stare at the wall? Have you lost interest in doing the things that you once loved? Feeling uninspired can be the result of sadness, grief, and loss, but it can also be a sign that you're stuck. Is fear holding you back from doing what's best for you? Are other people's opinions holding you back? Find a way to overcome your fears, make a change, and prepare for a shift.

- **You feel confused.** A major life decision can be overwhelming and we often see both sides of the coin—the good and bad—equally. This causes us to feel stuck in confusion. Try this: Close your eyes and envision the yes and the no to your question. Which feels lighter, brighter, and more peaceful? Go with that answer. Always. Be prepared for the answer to be the scariest and most difficult to accept.

- **You can't commit to anything.** Do you pursue something only to bail when it gets serious? Better to work through this now and save yourself the grief—something is wrong and needs fixing. So fix it. Be brave and take small steps towards your goal.

- **You're uncomfortable with the status quo.** Signs that you need a change in your life can show up in different ways. It can manifest as anger, sadness, and anxiety. It can also appear as a longing for something different, and jealousy or envy of others. If you're uncomfortable with the status quo, make change by bringing your attention to when you feel angry, sad, or anxious. Once you identify the thing that is causing your pain and needs to change, don't be afraid to take the steps to change it. Set your intention on something better.

Know how to reignite your job search. Once you realize that you are no longer in love with your job, you need to figure out what to do next, and, most importantly, how to keep yourself happy during the process. Navigating a career change isn't easy, but here are some ideas to keep it as smooth as possible.

- **Create a life outside of work.** Don't let work be the only thing that is important in your life. Explore the city you're in and find things that allow you to have something to look forward to. Join a cooking class or a book club. Find a hobby for your spare time.

- **Don't be afraid to talk.** Let your close friends and family know you are looking for a career change. Maybe they have some introductions they could make or suggestions for possible opportunities? Contact the college you attended and see how long you have access to its career center. Sit down with an advisor who can help you tweak your resume. Consult with friends. Conduct informational interviews with professionals you know.

- **Look for mentors at your work.** Talk to people you admire. Get ideas from people you trust about how they have gone about their job path.

- **Set goals and work toward them each week.** Map out a plan to get you through your career change. Set attainable goals and do something each week to accomplish them.

- **Set a date for when you want to leave.** Pick a month as a deadline for your exit. This will help you realize that you really are making the change, and it will give you a little push toward getting your job search going.

- **But don't leave your job until you have the next one lined up.** Don't find out the hard way that employers prefer to hire people who already have a job. Too many gaps in your resume can raise a red flag for potential employers.

Position yourself in a changing landscape. What does the "new economy" mean for you and your career? The landscape of getting (and keeping) a job is changing, so you need to pay attention to avoid being left behind. Job seekers need to change the way they talk to employers.

Ask yourself the following questions to keep up with the changing times.

- **How can I add value?** In a *New York Times* op-ed piece by Thomas Friedman entitled "How to Get a Job" (see end-of-chapter resource list), Harvard education expert Tony Wagner is quoted on the new paradigm of finding employment: "The world doesn't care what you know, all it cares about is what you can do with what you know." The good news for everyone in today's new world of work is that it's not about where you got your education or how you learned your skills, but about the value you can add to a project or organization.

- **Do I have the skills?** Today's marketplace is less focused on academic credentials than it is on matching the right skill set with the available work opportunity. This isn't to say you should skip college or graduate school, if you think they are right for you, but the degrees they confer are not enough in today's competitive world of work. Identify the skills you need and then set out to acquire them. Read books in your own time, build relationships with others who are doing similar work, find mentors to guide you on your path, and look for opportunities to gain and practice those skills.

Don't rule out the idea of changing fields. Is it possible to find work in an industry in which you have no experience? The answer is yes. You can definitely move into a new sector and make the case that your skills are transferable. It's never too late to switch fields. The transition can even be easier than you would think—and definitely spark some excitement in your career and your life.

That said, starting your job search in a new field can be intimidating; you may feel like employers won't be interested in you due to what they assume is your irrelevant background and work experience. Your job is to show that your background can still be an asset to your potential employer.

- **Volunteer.** Look for ways to show people what you can do. Join an advisory committee, sign up to help manage an annual dinner, or work on a fundraising drive. This will let leaders see your work firsthand and build important relationships.

- **Network and do informational interviews.** Remember what you learned about this earlier in this guide? It's just as applicable for changing fields as it is to looking for a new job. Reaching out to experts is a great way to find out about the field you hope to enter. Many of the people you meet will also have seen others make the transition into their sector from a different one. Ask what strategies have worked or not worked as they've watched others crack a new field—or better yet, hired such people. And don't forget about professional groups and industry events. Almost every industry or occupation has a professional association. (See the end-of-chapter resource list in Chapter 3 for a variety of links to these kinds of groups.)

- **Don't discredit your experience.** Once you begin interviewing in a new field, do not dismiss your own experience—even if it doesn't feel relevant. Every professional experience has value. Recently the hiring manager at Edelman Public Relations in Portland shared a story with the Mac's List staff about someone she interviewed who related her experience as a barista to skills needed in a public relations job. She ended up hiring the barista for a paid internship, based on the case she made. If you can relate your work experience to skills you will need in a future job, it is always valuable.

- **Highlight your personal interests.** Your personal life can always boost an employer's opinion of you. Don't be afraid to share what your hobbies and interests are—especially if they demonstrate your creativity or drive. Examples of interests to discuss with an employer might include blogging, photography, running marathons, or volunteering in community events or organizations. Just make sure to focus on how your interests display positive characteristics about you as a potential employee.

Decide whether graduate school is right for you.

As mentioned previously, today's economy is more focused on skills and results than on academic credentials and degrees. Yet in some cases, the decision to go to graduate school can reap a wide variety of benefits, both for you as an individual and for your long-term career path as well.

Answer these questions before deciding to apply. Consider the following before you decide to invest your precious time and money in the pursuit of a graduate degree.

- **Do you want to switch fields?** Getting a degree may be the only path to that new career, or it may be a big shortcut to years of piecing together relevant work experience. Informational interviews with connections in your desired field can help you decide whether going back to school is necessary.

- **What is needed for promotion and job security in your field?** In certain careers, advancement and growth are not possible without additional certification, training, degrees, or licenses. Continuing education can pave the way for advancement by giving you new skills and keeping you informed of new trends in your industry. It can also pave a path for a different job or a promotion.

- **Is it worth the time commitment?** It's always better financially for you to get your degree while still working, but that requires a lot of juggling and a fair amount of lost sleep. Do some soul-searching, evaluate your available time, look at your financial situation, and assess whether you can afford to go to graduate school full or part time. Ask yourself, "Is the long-term benefit worth the sacrifices I'll be making?" It is important to evaluate the costs of going back to school and the potential return on your investment.

Know how graduate school can help you. If you decide to go, here are a few of the benefits you can expect to receive.

- **Updated skills:** Your writing improves dramatically when faced with the red pen marks of a professor. You'll also do dozens of presentations, which will boost your public speaking skills. Finally, you'll gain confidence from being surrounded by peers in your field and sharing information and ideas with them.

- **A knowledge of new trends:** Any program worth its salt is doing everything it can to keep ahead of the trends and to train its students to be innovators in the field. You'll likely attend workshops led by top minds and local leaders in your field as part of your program's courses and extracurricular events.

- **An expanded professional network:** You'll meet many people in the community doing great work in your chosen field. Build relationships, connect on LinkedIn, meet for coffee to discuss shared interests—whatever you do—leverage relationships with your classmates, your professors, and guest speakers. It *will* pay off.

Consider local alternatives to graduate school. Maybe you just need a few courses to add or brush up on skills or some additional training to show you've mastered a specific skill set. Here are some areas to explore instead of undertaking a complete graduate school program.

- **Professional certificates:** Portland State University offers many options in professional development from a certificate in digital marketing strategies to human resource management. At the Institute for Nonprofit Management, some courses may even be taken a la carte.

- **Professional workshops and endorsements:** Weekend workshops like those at the University of Oregon are a great resource for professional development. Also check out the endorsements at Pacific Northwest College of Art.
- **Community courses:** Portland Community College offers a wide range of classes from how to use Excel to Grant Writing at an affordable cost.

Don't be afraid to mix it up.

As noted above, many experts view job security as an outmoded concept. A truly risk-free career comes from knowing that your skills are marketable and transferable to a variety of projects and positions. In Chapter 7 we discussed self-employment and how many people put together different projects to create a career or business. Combinations of projects like these are often referred to as a portfolio career.

What is a portfolio career? In its simplest form, a portfolio career is one that allows you to combine a variety of projects, paid and unpaid, to create full-time work for yourself that may be more meaningful than a single full-time job with just one employer. Examples of activities that can be part of a portfolio career are part-time jobs, freelance projects, temporary jobs, contract positions, volunteer opportunities, and full-time self-employment.

When should I consider a portfolio career? Laura Schlafly, founder of Career Choices with Laura and a frequent contributor to the *Mac's List* blog, often writes about portfolio careers and midlife job seekers. (See more of her advice later in this chapter.) She suggests considering a portfolio career in the following situations...

...if you're frustrated with your current employer.

...if you're starting your career.

...if you're seeking less stressful work.

...if you're self-employed or starting your own business.

...if you're unemployed and need paid work.

...if you're retired but would like to keep working at a paying job.

...if you're balancing other responsibilities but want paid work.

What are the benefits of a portfolio career? For people who are self-motivated, energetic, and not afraid of risk, a portfolio career is a good option for the following reasons. It is the best way to diffuse employment risk while diversifying your sources of income. The flexibility that comes from stepping outside the nine-to-five routine gives you more options and more freedom. You learn the value of your skills in the market and are able to put a price tag on them. There is the excitement that comes from moving from one engaging project to the next. And you may feel more ownership and emotional investment in your projects when you are working for yourself.

What is the downside to a portfolio career? As with full-time self-employment, portfolio careers are a good fit for people who manage time well and are multi-taskers. People who like structure, routine, and hierarchy may find a portfolio career difficult to sustain emotionally. Its disadvantages include a certain amount of financial risk, the potential for stress when deadlines collide, and uncertainty about what is coming down the line tomorrow, next week, next month, and next year.

What strategies do I need to create a successful portfolio career? If you decide a portfolio career is right for you, Laura suggests considering the following options and ideas to help ease the way.

- **Build at least six months of savings to support any startup costs.** Not even high-wire aerialists like working without a net.

- **Take a starter position in one or more of your areas of interest.** This allows you to earn some income while learning and exploring. There is no need to stay too long in any one role or company. This is a valuable baby step and works especially well for folks who have lower living costs and can afford the risk.

- **Work part time in your current job or field to cover your basic living costs, such as your rent or mortgage.** Then focus your remaining time in real portfolio research. Take this time to try on your possibilities and find out what calls to you.

- **Throw caution to the wind and take the leap. Risky?** You bet, especially if you have dependents. So you'll probably feel more at ease if you also create a Plan B to turn to if at first you don't succeed. This all-or-nothing approach requires laser focus and abundant self-motivation, in addition to knowing your dependable strengths, those natural talents you have.

- **Make sure you have the support you need.** That means emotional support from family, friends, and collegues; developmental support from peers such as mentors or career experts; promotional support from people who will share their connections and introduce you to key people in your field; and material support from service providers and financiers as needed.

What TV Detective Columbo Can Teach Boomers about Job Hunting

by **Laura Schlafly** Founder of Career Choices with Laura and Licensed Spiritual Practitioner at Life Choices with Laura

If you're over fifty, you probably remember the 1970s series starring Peter Falk as homicide detective Lt. Columbo. Every episode began with a crime and we all knew the perpetrator from scene one. The thrill was watching Columbo solve the case, clue by clue. Here's how to use four of Columbo's techniques to solve your own job-search case.

1. **Don't cast a wide net.** If you are sixty today, you may work another twenty-five or more years. People look back twenty-five years and say, "That happened fast!" Ask yourself: "Will the next twenty-five years happen that fast? If so, what is my purpose? When will I live my best life?" By the time you hit midlife, you have expertise in many areas. Search for a job only after you know what you want. Research jobs that fit, but don't apply until you've defined what you want. This applies to everything, from custom crafting your resume, to tapping the extensive network you've developed across the years, to targeting the companies you want to work for and the people you want to interrogate—I mean interview. Single-minded focus is the key. Columbo started with the outcome, then found the clues that led to it.

2. **Look for firms with problems you can solve.** If you're over fifty, you have the expert knowledge an employer needs. This is your advantage over younger workers. Find companies facing challenges where your experience

gives you an edge. While posing as a bumbling gumshoe, Columbo asked basic but strategic questions. In the end, his knowledge and persistence nailed the case.

3. **Consider an "encore" career.** Columbo was famous for pretending to leave and then coming back for many "encores," always saying, "Just one more thing …" Many older job seekers turn to an encore career at the end of their professional lives. An encore career may mean reentering the workforce in a different capacity or with different skills. It could mean self-employment— according to a Kaufman Foundation Report, people aged fifty-five to sixty-four start approximately 10,000 new businesses each month. Or it might be some combination of part-time work, self-employment, and volunteering. Don't be afraid to mix and match in a way that works for you.

4. **Repeat steps 1 through 3.** Columbo always kept after the suspect. He was pestering them, but your strategy is persisting. It's easy to give up after a rejection and focus on the negative. Keep it positive by using neutral statements such as "another person was selected" and remembering that you are one step closer to a "yes." It's not a crime to get a "no," but it's *criminal* not to keep at it.

Don't ever stop learning.

As you navigate your career across the years, stay on top of current trends and news in your field. One easy way to do that is to follow blogs about careers in general and about work in your chosen area specifically. Bloggers are passionate by nature—you need amazing energy and focus to keep posting week after week. Take a lesson from them and lavish the same time and effort on your career path.

Follow these blogs! The following are some of our favorite job-related blogs here at Mac's List. Many of them originate in Oregon, and some of the writers mentioned contribute to our own blog. Some have been referenced in other chapters, but here they are in one neat and tidy package.

- **Ask a Manager**: Before striking out as a consultant, Alison Green was chief of staff for a medium-sized organization. Every day she answers questions about workplace and job search topics.

- **InternMatch:** Jenny Xie posts several times a week about topics of interest to interns and college students, including tips about landing internships and making the most of them. The InternMatch site includes hundreds of internship openings across the country.

- **Career Beavers:** Written by the staff of the Office of Career Services at the Oregon State University (OSU), this blog serves OSU students and grads but offers excellent information for any job seeker.

- **Jobhuntercoach:** Arnie Fertig lives in New England where he ran his own recruiting company for ten years. He now helps people master the skills they need for focused job searches and shares what he learned as a recruiter via weekly blog posts.

- **Kontrary:** Rebecca Thorman blogs from Washington, DC, on how to navigate your career, money, and life so that "you can find meaningful work, enjoy the heck out of it, and earn more money."

- **Life After College:** Jenny Blake is an author and career and business coach in New York City. A former Google employee, Jenny and her team write about life, careers, goals, and relationships with a special focus on issues of interest to twenty-somethings.

- **Launch Yourself:** A "reformed corporate drone," Melissa Anzman lives in Colorado and is "passionate about helping late twenty- to forty-some-things make their dream job." Her blog offers resources to help people choose their own career path.

- **PDXMindshare:** Founded by Anvil Media's Kent Lewis, PDXMindshare is one of Portland's best online sources for jobs. It also features an excellent blog that aggregates content from national career sites.

- **Penelope Trunk:** A founder of Brazen Careerist, a career site for professionals, Penelope writes regularly about career-management and job-search issues of interest to Generation Y.

And don't forget the blogs by some of our local experts! Many of them write their own blogs or contribute frequently to others' blogs.

- **JobJenny.com:** Jenny Foss is a career strategist and the voice of the popular career blog JobJenny.com. Jenny also operates a Portland-based recruiting agency and is the author of the *Ridiculously Awesome Resume Kit* and the *Ridiculously Awesome LinkedIn Kit*. You may find Jenny on Twitter @JobJenny.

- **Pathfinder Writing and Career Services**: Speaker, author, and resume writer Dawn Rasmussen works from Portland, Oregon. Dawn's blog offers ideas and tools people can use to manage their careers and find fulfilling jobs.
- **Career Enlightenment**: An Oregon-based social media expert, Joshua Waldman writes for job seekers looking for comprehensive information about conducting a job search online.
- **Back of the Brain**: Portland-based Jungian psychotherpist Satya Byock writes about psychotherapy and dream work. Her practice is devoted to helping individuals navigate the first quarter of life.
- **Story Water**: Jen Violi is a Portland-based author, editor, and writing coach. Her blog is about the healing power of story.
- **Career Transition**: The Inside Job: Vicki Lind contributes to this blog written by locally based career coaches, resume writers, and career counselors.
- **Coaching for Clarity**: Aubrie De Clerck helps you open doors to fulfilling work.
- **Career Choices with Laura**: Laura Schlafly is dedicated to guiding midlife professionals through career detours and helping them navigate their second-act careers.
- **Career Factors**: Founder of Portland-based Career Factors, Marsha Warner, SPHR, is an executive recruiter and career coach. She teaches groups and works individually with clients in career transition. She also speaks at local job-search groups and has published on the topics of career management, recruiting, and career renewal.

Dig deeper!

For links to some of the topics covered in this chapter (including getting unstuck, professional workshops, the changing job market, the role of hobbies in a search, and Mr. Plywood, among many others), go to www.macslist.org/references.

You've reached

The End

of our book but we are confident
that with what you've learned
you'll shortly be starting on

The Beginning

of a great new job in Portland!
Good luck and let us know how it goes!
(Please use the following few pages for notes.)

The Mac's List Team
info@macslist.org

ISBN: 978-0-9909551-2-2

"The most difficult thing is the decision to act,
the rest is merely tenacity."

Amelia Earhart

*"One important key to success is self-confidence.
An important key to self-confidence is preparation."*

Arthur Ashe

"I was once afraid of people saying, 'Who does she think she is?' Now I have the courage to stand and say, 'This is who I am.'"

Oprah

If you're going through hell, keep going."

Winston Churchill

_____

Made in the USA
Lexington, KY
18 May 2017